PUT YOUR MOUTH

WHERE THE MONEY IS!

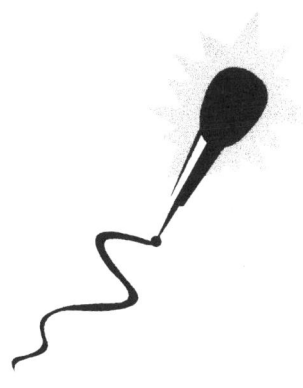

PUT YOUR MOUTH WHERE THE MONEY IS!

How To Build A Successful Radio and TV Voiceover Business

By Radio & Television Voiceover Personality
Sunny Quinn

Airwave Publications
P.O. Box 753
Jupiter, Florida 33468-0753

E-mail: sunnyq@juno.com

ISBN 0-9660531-0-9

Library of Congress Catalog Card Number: 97-94503
Quinn, Sunny
Put Your Mouth Where The Money Is

AIRWAVE PUBLICATIONS

 ACKNOWLEDGMENTS

I must take a moment to thank my colleagues who took a chance on me in the early days of my career and showed faith in my abilities. I will never forget the opportunities you have offered me and will always be appreciative of what you have done for my broadcasting and voiceover career. It is for that reason I wrote this book. You have inspired me to turn around and offer a hand up to those now getting started in the business.

I want to also acknowledge the contributing participants of the audio portion of this training kit. A big fat thank you goes to Bob Harper, Jim Austin, Russell Warner, Roland J. Norio, Gary Travers, Corey Marin, Steve Stansell, Joanne Rice, Claudia Potamkin, Linda Rocafort, and Sean Brady. You all have my deepest gratitude for your contributions, and my respect for your outstanding talent and professionalism.

Another big fat thank you goes to Rich Dickerson for being my radio mentor and friend, and also for the use of the ZZR studios; Rob Smith of Young, Fast & Scientific for your designing expertise on the book covers and web site; and Maurice Rodriguez for your expert photography on the outer front cover. You're the best!

THANK YOU!

(A big fat thank you)

DEDICATION

I dedicate this effort to those who stood by me with endless love, support, patience, understanding and encouragement throughout my career. I especially thank my husband, Don Brewer, for the love and encouragement during my entire broadcasting career; my daughter, Dale, for her tireless drilling to rid me of my New York accent; Ma for having me, which proved to be an invaluable beginning; my brother, Bill, for believing in everything I have ever done; my cat, E.T., for providing calming comfort by purring on my lap throughout the writing process; my other cat, Bear, for adding hundreds of blank pages to my documents by walking all over the keyboard as I wrote; and my dog, Alex, for providing me with a well-deserved break from the computer by needing to whiz every few hours. I love you all.

CONTENTS

INTRODUCTION

Stop talking for a minute and listen! Have you ever noticed how many different things in this world have a voice behind them? Let's see...radio and television commercials, television announcements, telephone answering machines, voice menus on phone systems, computer programs, instructional videos, corporate videos, company training tapes, audio books, cartoon characters, in-flight instruction and entertainment, infomercials, educational film strips, talking exhibits, CD-ROM computer games, software tutorials, and on...and on...and on.

Everywhere you go, everywhere you turn, you'll hear a voice. It may welcome you, direct you, instruct you, educate you, or entertain you. Voices are everywhere! Ever think that maybe one of those voices could be *yours*? Why not! With proper training and practice, like anything else, that *could* be your voice on the next travelogue video or TV commercial you watch!

Being a freelance voiceover talent is creative, fun, challenging, unique, unpredictable, respectable, and very rewarding. You get to be your own boss, make your own schedule, travel around, meet talented new people, work in different recording studios with lots of different talent, and hear your own voice on TV and radio.

This training kit offers you the information you will need to launch a brand new career...or enhance the one you have already started. I will share with you everything I have learned the hard way! Here are just some of the topics we will explore:

* How voiceovers can fit into your busy life
* How and where to get voice work
* How to train, utilize and care for your voice
* How to interpret and read commercial copy
* Studio etiquette
* Terminology
* Diction, articulation, proper pronunciation
* How to set up your business
* How to make a demo tape
* How to market yourself
* Setting talent fees
* Invoicing and collecting
* How to secure repeat business

The nature of the voiceover business can vary dramatically depending on your area and market size, so we will tackle all the issues from the middle. Utilize your common sense to adjust to your market size. For example, a commercial in Miami may pay $200. That same spot in Wyoming may pay only $30. In LA, you will need to audition for much of your work. In Kansas, the producer will simply call you and ask you to come in. For our purposes, we live in a medium market with a medium amount of available work, for a medium amount of money. Now get to work!

①

How I Stumbled Into The Voiceover Biz

HOW I STUMBLED INTO THE VOICEOVER BIZ

Much of my adult life was spent dabbling in various occupations, some more seriously than others. I made a fair living at all of them and I even enjoyed most of my jobs. The irony as I sit here writing this is that for decades, it never even *occurred* to me to use my voice to make a living. I've been a fashion designer, a retail boutique manager, a licensed cosmetologist, a lay midwife, and even a neonatal intensive care registered nurse. People had been telling me all my life they thought I had a nice voice. I thanked them for the very kind compliment, and went on my way.

Some number of years ago, my daughter, Dale, and I were vagabonding in a van around New England and ran into some old friends who were working on a muppet-type TV pilot. They asked me to "park it" for a few weeks and help them with set and costume design. I stayed to help out and while I was stationed in New Haven, Connecticut, I began listening to a local morning radio program, "Smith and Barber," on WPLR. I got completely hooked on these whackos!

Some time passed and the TV show wrapped up. I got an apartment and a job as a private duty nurse for a doctor's daughter in his home. Well, every morning at 8:00, these two radio goons would play the theme song to the old TV show *Flipper*, and they would run through a bit where they called Flipper and fed him his breakfast (great sound effects, I might add). After they fed Flipper, I knew it was time for me to leave for work. One day, 8:00 passed, then 8:20, and they still hadn't fed Flipper. Obviously at that point, I was late for work! I called the radio station and asked them why they had neglected to feed poor Flipper. They thanked me for the reminder and humbly admitted their negligence, and then asked if I would like to help them sing the Flipper theme song over the phone, which of course was played over the air. Also to make amends, they invited me down to their studios the following morning to personally feed Flipper his breakfast.

The next morning at the WPLR studio was my first real on-air experience. I not only got to meet Brian and Bruce and Flipper, but I had an incredible eye-opening experience. I left there thinking "These guys get *paid* to do that...I'm definitely in the wrong business!"

Later that year, I moved to South Florida. The smartest and very first thing I did was enroll at the Connecticut School of Broadcasting. I landed my first radio job the day after graduation at WYFX, Foxy 1040. I also did my very first radio commercial voiceover that week ...for money! I just couldn't believe it! I left that studio with fifty bucks in my hand, just for reading a *minute's* worth of words!

Only four months later I was offered a position in morning drive as a sidekick and News/Public Affairs Director at WNGS, Lite 92.1 FM. In addition to a whole bunch of freelance voiceovers during my six years there, I hosted three television shows and numerous TV commercials. One unfortunate day, the radio station was sold. I then moved across town to WEAT,

Sunny 104.3 FM. I created an evening love song and dedication program called "Sunny After Dark" which quickly went to number one. In addition, I hosted a Sunday Jazz Brunch, and then finished out my time there in middays. After four years, I was offered a great opportunity to be the only solo female morning driver at a local rock station, WZZR 92.7 FM.

That's how it all began. So now, this is what *I* do for a living...just like those whacked-out radio guys in New Haven! And you know the best part? It could happen to *you!* That, my friend, is exactly why I've written this book.

2

The Wonderful World of Voiceovers

THE WONDERFUL WORLD OF VOICEOVERS

Very few professions in this world can boast the diversity that the voiceover business can. Every day and every session is delightfully different than the one before. For the creative or restless soul, this can be the ultimate professional gift.

By purchasing this training kit, you obviously already have a curiosity or an interest in the industry. Maybe you're just exploring the possibilities. Maybe you know someone making a good living doing voiceovers. Maybe you've just landed your first or second radio job, and are seeking ways to boost your income. Maybe you've had a little experience in the voiceover biz, and you want to expand your opportunities and make it more profitable. Maybe you have another gig and just want to have fun while making a few bucks on the side. Maybe you hate laying drywall, and you're looking for a total career change.

The voiceover world has a great advantage because it can usually be molded to fit into *your* lifestyle and busy schedule. Most studios and clients are quite flexible with their time, and will work around your availability. I've worked all different day parts on the air, and none have adversely affected the quantity of business that comes my way. When I was on the air in morning drive time, they booked me for afternoon sessions. When I worked afternoons or evenings, I did all my recording in the morning hours. I'm not saying I have never lost a job because of my unavailability, but if they want *my* voice, they have to work with my available hours. Situations do arise where the client is under an urgent deadline I cannot accommodate, and therefore have to forfeit the job. Keep in mind if you plan to keep a full time job and add voiceovers as a second job, in all fairness you must make yourself available during *some* business hours.

This is generally a supplemental job. Unless you live in a large market and you have an overabundance of talent just oozing from your pores, it is best to "keep your day job!" Like many businesses, it has peaks and valleys, oases and droughts, times of prosperity and times of total bust. You may be booked every day for months and think you've got this knocked. Then the phone stops ringing. Was it something you did or said? Did you lose your talent? Did you forget your deodorant? No. The new work just temporarily stopped coming in. Maybe the clients shot their advertising wads on a recent holiday, or they're saving it for one upcoming. Maybe the client saves the largest portion of their limited advertising budget for tourist season. Maybe they changed their advertising campaign and no longer need for your voice. Maybe they felt it was time to try a new approach and go with a male instead of a female, or a female instead of a male. Maybe the studio likes to rotate their talent pool. The point is, the reason usually is logical, not personal. It's the nature of the beast. The work comes and the work goes. It will be to your benefit to brace yourself for the flow of the tide. In most markets, it is best to keep your voiceover business as your icing on the cake, not your bread and butter!

There are several ways to break into the business, but I have found that the vast majority of "voices" got their start in radio. It is a logical (but not essential) beginning. Many freelance jobs come from being heard on the air. It also gives you clout and credibility when marketing yourself to new clients or studios. They assume that if you are on the air, you have experience and training, and probably a decent voice. On a rare occasion it could actually work against you. Some feel that radio personalities sound too "announcerish" on commercials and do not possess a good, natural demeanor. However, many on-air personalities have done so well in the voiceover business that they depart from their radio jobs and take on voiceover work full time. It is certainly a very unique and colorful way to make a living in this world! Keep in mind, though, this is possible only in the larger markets of this country. Generally there is not enough available voice work in smaller markets to sustain a full time salary, but it sure can beef up that modest salary you've been living with!

As with most everything worth attaining in this world, establishing yourself in this crazy business takes drive, desire, determination, time and lots of footwork. The best part is when you succeed, it is all your own doing. You are the one who called the shots along the way. It is your own hard work that reaps the results. It is a business that takes very little start-up capital, but can reap very big financial rewards.

Some of the most delightful and creative people can be found in the world of voiceovers. I have seen great friendships and long-lasting working relationships evolve from being in "the talent loop." You meet self-motivated, creative and confident professionals...many of them real characters! These people make work fun and enjoyable. I have yet to ever dread going to work! I have looked forward to each and every recording session I have ever been fortunate enough to land. How many people can say that about their jobs?

It would probably be in your best interest to read this training material in its entirety to get a good overview and feel for where you are headed. Then go back and begin applying the different elements as you need them. Keep in mind you need to adapt them to your location, market size, availability, skill level and talent.

Two of the audio cassettes are targeted for later, after you have a good feel for the basics. They offer advice from the pros about how to further your career and give examples of good voiceover demo tapes. The tape labeled "practice cassette" is for your use throughout your training.

This is a journey into the world of voiceovers. Enjoy your trip...it is a great world. Most of all, have *fun* at what you do. It's rare.

3

Types of Voiceover Work

TYPES OF VOICEOVER WORK

This is truly a profession in which the sky is the limit. If you've got what it takes...talent, drive and imagination, it can take you wherever you want to go. Let's take a look at just a *few* of the many possibilities.

COMMERCIALS

The average American is exposed to literally thousands and thousands of radio and television commercials. These ads run locally, regionally, nationally and even internationally. The ads for local businesses are usually produced on a local level, meaning *you* get the opportunity to do the voice work for them. They are usually done at a local production studio or radio station, then distributed for airing around your area. This is a big advantage if you live in a small to medium market. If you are in a large market, chances are many of the regional and national spots are produced near you. This offers even more opportunity to get bigger jobs for bigger money.

TELEVISION BOOTH ANNOUNCING

Sit down in front of your television for half an hour, and count the times you hear a voice without an on-camera person speaking. The majority of that is called "booth announcing." This refers to the brief promotional announcements you hear, like "Tonight at 8" or "This Sunday night at 9" or "And now, we return to the Movie of the Week" or "Previously on Melrose Place."

You get the idea. Well, someone was hired to go into the studio or TV station and record those brief identifiers and promotional liners. It's a fun job, and can be very lucrative when you get into a situation where you go back in and record updates every week!

RADIO AND TELEVISION STATION VOICES
If you listen closely for a period of time to your favorite radio or TV station, you'll begin to notice a familiar voice. Every time there is a break or a station identifier or promotional blurb, it's the same voice. Someone has nailed down the job of "the station voice." This person does all the voice work for that particular station...from legal ID's to identity sweepers, from return liners to promotional mentions. For example, near the top of every hour on radio you will hear "WEAT FM, West Palm Beach" or "WZZR, Stuart." That is a legal ID required hourly by the Federal Communications Commission, and recorded by the station voice. That voice may also do something like "You're listening to Sunny 104.3 for today's hits and yesterday's favorites." You may also recognize something like "You're rockin' with Denny James, on 92.7 ZZR."

Make it a point to listen for them. If you have never noticed them before, you will now! The Program Director and/or the Production Director at radio and TV stations listen to dozens and dozens of voice demos, and choose the voice that best suits their station. There are recording studios around the country that specialize in producing station voices. Media consultants may also recommend a certain voice for a station, and more times than not, the "voice" lives and works outside of that market...thus, opening a whole new world! Your voice could be on that station down in Tucson or up in Buffalo!

INDUSTRIAL & CORPORATE VIDEOS AND CD's
This is a fast-growing industry. More and more businesses of all sizes are finding that it's easier to reach more people with information more efficiently through the use of videos and computer CD-ROM's. These are known in the field as "industrials," and a great source of voice work. Think for a moment of all the possibilities...new employee training tapes or introductory tapes, "how-to" videos, new product introductions, step-by-step instructional tapes, travelogue videos that sell vacation resorts, computer software program training, facility introductions, or college and university tutorials. Just look at the "how-to" shelf at your local video store and you'll see what I mean! If you are a good cold reader, this is a great opportunity to make great money! You go into a recording session, sit down and read for a period of time, and get paid hundreds of dollars! We'll discuss setting fees a bit later, but you can pull in a good week's pay in one afternoon!

EDUCATIONAL VIDEOS, CASSETTES, CD's
Educational videos, training audio cassettes, and computer CD-ROM's are also exploding in usage. There are numerous voiceover jobs available for college videos, explaining everything from nursing techniques to internet surfing. Lots of mail order educational courses

are also done on videos, cassettes, or computer CD-ROM's. Any format utilized for software tutorials, medical procedures, technical procedures, "how-to's" etc., need *someone* to voice them. This is a huge area, and well worth investigating in your area!

TELECOMMUNICATIONS

The 90's will always have bragging rights as being a decade of huge advancement in sophisticated telecommunications. How many times have you called a mail order business or a doctor's office or the Motor Vehicle Department, and the first thing you hear is a voice menu. "If you'd like to place an order, press 1 now." Someone was paid to sit there and record all those options. I do the voice menu for a local cable company, and they like to update frequently as their business expands...so guess who gets called in to make those changes? Many businesses will do their own, but many come to find out that you get what you pay for! They usually end up calling in the pros to do the voice work properly and professionally.

The possibilities for voice menus and message-on-hold are far too vast to even mention here, but allow me to get your imaginative juices flowing. How about car dealerships, movie theatres, community playhouses, hospitals, medical offices and complexes, corporations, mail order houses, government offices, libraries, schools and universities, entertainment complexes, retail businesses, video rental outlets, paging and telecommunications companies, or even your public zoo.

AUDIO BOOKS

Audio books, also known as talking books, are increasing in popularity due to the fact many folks are simply too busy these days to sit down and read. Audio books can just be popped into the cassette player in the car. Audio books are also extremely popular with frequent travelers. Those hours of flight time can be put to good use by listening to a great book. Let's not overlook the vast usage by the visually impaired population. Audio tapes are utilized for pleasure, inspiration, motivation and education...by all types of people in all professions...and what a great source of income for the voiceover talent!

MOTION PICTURE ANIMATED CHARACTERS

This is becoming a monster of an industry! With all the advancements the world is making in computer animation, it opens a vast new assortment of possibilities for the talented voiceover artist. Those with a talent in acting and character voices should investigate the options. It's staggering to look at the sophistication achieved over recent years in animated major motion pictures. Oh sure, they usually hire well-known actors for the lead roles, but look at the huge number of *support* roles in these films! These jobs are not an easy task to land, but this kind of talent can lead to a very exciting and lucrative career!

INFOMERCIALS

We've all had those late nights in front of the tube. We get to that point when the only thing on the air is yet another infomercial...you know, those half-hour or even hour-long commercials that take twenty minutes to even figure out that it *is* a commercial! I used to hate them until I realized I could make good money from them! If you can't lick 'em, join 'em. If you watch these programs, you'll notice that every ten or fifteen minutes, the camera will depart from the on-camera host and focus on the product. Then a voiceover explains the product, benefits, warrantees, guarantees, and how to order. Many video production houses actually specialize in infomercials, and should not be overlooked when setting up your client base!

COMPUTER SOFTWARE VOICEOVERS
Ah, the possibilities! If you're a computer hound, you know exactly what I'm referring to. Many programs have "built-in" voices that greet you, guide you, instruct you, educate you, and even say good-bye to you. Windows 95 has a voice. Many printer programs have a voice. The software programs are getting extremely sophisticated, utilizing the voice more than ever. Computer CD-ROM games integrate voices with the action constantly. There are CD-ROM production houses cropping up all over, and are definitely worth checking out.

IN-FLIGHT INSTRUCTION/ENTERTAINMENT
If you've flown a larger jet lately, you have probably noticed the flight attendants no longer need to stand in the aisle and personally demonstrate safety features to you. It's done on video. During the runway taxi time, monitors drop down and the safety video is shown to passengers. The great majority of that video is done in

voiceover mode. You will see someone demonstrate the equipment on screen, but the tutorial is primarily voiced over. Some airlines also present a promotional video following the safety tutorial. Again, they are done almost entirely in voiceover format.

4

Style and Delivery

STYLE AND DELIVERY

Now that you have an idea of just how vast this business is, it is time to focus on you and how to develop your talent. The style and delivery that you develop will be yours and yours alone. Your unique voiceover "personality" will become the reason the studio calls *you* to do the spot. However, there are several factors that have universal significance and influence regarding your voiceover delivery. Let's take a detailed look at the most important elements that affect your voice work.

VOICE

Your voice is your instrument...your tool of the trade. Take care of it! No voice, no job. Develop it, fine tune it, and nurture it. Become comfortable with listening to your voice on tape. It doesn't sound the same on tape as it does in your head. You need to get over that cringe factor and make peace with your voice so you can begin working with it. Detach yourself in order to critique it objectively. You can only correct yourself when you can recognize your faults.

Care for your voice just like you would any tool that is critical to your job. Voice villains include smoking, alcohol, caffeine, dry air, stress, and screaming or talking in noisy settings. Most of these are common sense, but are frequently ignored or overlooked. Laryngitis can bump you off the "available talent list" for weeks!

BREATHING

Proper breathing is vital to good speech communication. Remember, your breath is the driving force, the *engine*, that supplies your vocal sounds. Practice breathing deeply so you can read through your copy without a lot of interruptions for air. With practice, you should be able to read 15 or 20 seconds of copy before having to take a breath. It sounds much more natural to take a breath at the end of a sentence rather than in the middle. Also, fill up on air *off mike* right before your first spoken word. Give a pause between your breath and the first word so the breath can be easily edited out.

ARTICULATION AND DICTION

Articulation and diction relate to the clear, distinct sounds coming out of your mouth during a read. Let all those vowels and consonants have their moment in the sun! The vowels give the voice greater carrying power, while the consonants provide clear articulation. Your words should have a fluid, natural, and unaffected quality. These sounds will be the finished product of the lips, jaw, tongue, and soft palate all working together as "articulators." Keep in mind that speaking too fast can contribute to poor diction and decreased articulation.

PRONUNCIATION

Nothing sticks out like a wrong pronunciation of a word. We pick up lazy and poor speaking habits over time. This can have detrimental effects in the voice-over biz! Review the list of commonly mispronounced words found later in the book. Never be afraid to ask the client how he or she would like a word pronounced if you are not sure...*before* you begin your read.

INFLECTION

Inflection refers to the change in pitch, tone or intensity. Once you find your natural pitch range, it is easy to move up or down from that point with ease and effectiveness. Your natural pitch is where you generally begin normal conversation, with the appropriate volume and quality and with the least expenditure of energy. The intensity of your voice can be varied by the loudness or softness of your vocal delivery. These fluctuations should correspond to the logical and emotional meaning of the written copy. Your delivery should be understandable and colorful, and give meaning and significance to your material. Learn to develop and incorporate variety, melody, and emphasis in your words. Tonal quality is also critical to the overall quality of the spot. This is achieved through proper breathing control.

PITCH

Pitch simply refers to the highness or lowness of your voice and plays a critical role in the "listenability" of your voice. Someone with a pitch too high or low or even monotonous will always risk losing the listener entirely. High pitch can sometimes result from being over-anxious or nervous. High pitch also results in a loss of fullness of your voice's tone. The more relaxed your throat muscles, the more pleasant your vocal sounds. Too low a voice can usually be compensated for by using faster pacing. This tends to raise the pitch and can be a very useful tool of the trade.

Monotony is instant death. The spot will come across lifeless, dull, boring, and uninteresting. This is when it is critical to find your natural range so you have more room to fluctuate up or down from that neutral point. Listen to yourself on tape at regular intervals to check your pitch and inflection.

VOLUME
Natural vocal volume varies greatly from person to person. Speaking either too loudly or too softly becomes annoying to the listener. They will react by tuning out and breaking off the speaker/listener communication. However, variety of volume can add color and emphasis to your work. Try taping yourself in a group. You will know immediately whether your natural speaking voice is loud or soft compared to others. You can work on your self-adjustments from there.

PACING
Pacing becomes an integral part of your finished delivery. Pacing is a large contributor to the effectiveness of your work. A variance of your pace adds interest and emphasis to what you are saying. Imagine driving from Los Angeles to New York at sixty miles per hour

with no changes in speed or scenery. You'd be snoozing before you hit Las Vegas! Even professional runners vary their pacing for both energy conservation and interest. You need to inject enough variety to hold the interest of your listener.

Many times there will be a lot of written copy that needs to be squeezed into 30 or 60 seconds, so a quick pace is mandatory. On the other end of the spectrum, sometimes you need to buy time to reach the 60 second mark with very little copy. It's all in the pacing. You are looking at the finish line, and the vehicle to get you there is your copy and your voice. It is the pacing that will determine how close you come to the mark. Pacing is also a useful tool to get your pitch either up or down to where it should be. It should be comfortable to the listener's ear. If it is too fast, your listener will not be able to keep up with you, and valuable information is lost. If it is too slow, it becomes boring and the listener tends to drift. Either way, attention is lost.

A pause, on the other hand, can be a very useful "emphasizing" tool. The perfect pause is an art form. Pauses can attract attention as efficiently as a strong word or sentence. It gives your audience a moment to digest what you have said, to let it sink in, to absorb an important point. A good pause can also create a sense of anticipation. It can mark a transition or an introduction of a new idea. The right number of pauses, at the right moments, for the right amount of time, can be very effective. A pause also gives you time to catch your breath!

ENERGY

Different products will often instinctively dictate the energy level you will use for your delivery. Much of this is common sense. A big rock concert will naturally call for a more motivated, high energy read, while a vacation package on a remote getaway island will call for a calm and relaxed read. You want to give the read the same amount of energy that will be derived from the product itself. In most studio situations, if your energy level is not what the director had in mind, you will be asked to redo it with either a higher or lower energy delivery. This skill will sharpen over time.

SKILL

Natural talent is a gift. Developing that talent takes skill. Your skill in this business will directly determine how successful you will be. You never want to become complacent in your ability level. You want to keep up with the competition, keep sharp, and always keep challenged. Remember, it's not a great voice that makes you successful, it's the great things you can do with the voice you have.

Become a master of observation. Watch and listen to people. Discover their characterizations and mannerisms. Observe all the interesting dynamics between people and log it into your memory bank. One day you may end up having to play that character type in a commercial role!

Voiceover work is not just reading, it's acting. It takes skill and practice to become that character in the script and to portray it convincingly. If you are serious about your career, you should consider enrolling in acting or improvisational classes. When you translate those newly-learned skills into radio acting, you will be amazed how much depth and believability you can add to your performance behind the mike. Learn how to make a commitment to your character. Become that character in heart, body, mind, and soul. Give that character a life and an identity all its own. Learn to pretend and role play. Know where your character fits into the scheme of things in the spot, and act it out accordingly. Remember, *you* are not the star. Your *character* is the one that will make the copy and the product come alive.

EXPRESSION

We go back to the familiar old adage that best describes the nature of radio. It is the theatre of the mind. We do not have the use of visuals in the typical voiceover situation, so all modes of expression must come from the voice. In essence, it all comes down to *how* you say the words to get the meaning across effectively. You need to convey them with feeling and conviction, or your listener will not believe you. The listener should be able to "hear" your expressions, gestures, emotions and feelings. Take the simple example of a smile. Speak a sentence or two into a tape recorder with a straight face. Repeat the same lines, only this time put a big smile on your face. Hear the difference? Your smile can actually be heard!

When a read calls for some emotion other than a smile, try to place yourself in a situation that creates that emotion in your mind. Try to recall when you last experienced that emotion and relive it. These emotions may include excitement, fright, hunger, cold, heat, thirst, pain, or grief. Place yourself there and express the emotion through your voice. Hand and facial gestures greatly add to the expression in your voice. You may look like an idiot and feel like a fool, but you'll be called back because of your convincing and expressive role-playing.

PERSONALITY

Personality plays a big role in the success of your voiceover business. This is the one aspect that is all yours. This is what makes you different from all the other talent in the field. You can learn the same basic skills as everyone else, but it is *you* that you bring into the studio. Your own personality, lifestyle, and life experiences all enter the picture and have an effect on the finished product. Become familiar with your personality and how it is projected into your work. Use it to your advantage, both in your voiceover skills and in your working relationships. Your personality can even become a marketing tool for your business to be utilized as a unique edge over other talent.

DIALECT

Dialect is that little flavor in your voice that is a dead giveaway of where you were raised! How about that good ol' New York accent, or the unique Boston accent, or the sweet southern drawl. Each has a distinctive style and attraction all its own. The problem is, you don't want to necessarily be identified by your dialect. Professional reads are usually very generic when it comes to dialect. Localization of dialect detracts from the versatility and universal appeal of the spot. The challenge for you is getting that "New York" or "Boston" or "Georgia" out of your mouth! Old habits die hard, and it takes a lot of drilling and repeating those tough words over and over again on tape. Incorporate your polished pronunciations into everyday conversation and practice, practice, practice! It's hard, but I also *know* it's possible. I'm from New Yawk!

CHARACTER VOICES

Here is a rule of thumb. If you cannot do a character well, don't do it at all! This is a fast-lane approach to making a real idiot of yourself and it happens all the time. Some people are very talented and all their characters seem to just spew forth in everyday conversation. Those characters can be put to work. Some need to work on their characters to perfect them. Others think they are good and they are not. I am sure you have heard spots on the air that sound phony and amateurish. More times than not, they have tried to incorporate character voices that just do not work.

However, if you are a talented character actor, you are a hot commodity. Diverse talent translates into more work. You could land a spot where you play two or three different roles rather than the studio calling in three different people. Just imagine the career possibilities in animated major motion pictures!

 SELF-TEST

It may help you to run through this quick self-analysis of your voice, style, and delivery. Usually we are our own worst enemies and can benefit from our self-critique. The goal is not perfection, but improvement!

1. My first impression when I listen back to my voice on a tape recorder is _____.

2. The thing I like most about my voice is _____.

3. The thing I would most like to change about my voice is _____.

4. Other people tell me my voice is _____.

5. The area in which I need to work the hardest is
   _____.

6. When I get behind a microphone, I _____.

7. People seem to (have) (have no) trouble understanding my speech in normal conversation.

8. I describe my own delivery of speech to be
   a) average   b) animated   c) monotone
   d) motivating   e) annoying   f) intriguing

5

Pest Control

PEST CONTROL

The English language is a beautiful thing, but it is infested with pesky, devilish little words that must be exterminated! A very important factor that will separate the pros from the large field of amateurs is the mastery of the English language. You must strive to become an expert in the use of language.

The following is a list of many pesky words that are commonly mispronounced, whether from laziness or ignorance. Sloppy or lazy articulation could cost you the next job! Be careful to include each syllable, vowel, and consonant. Also get in the habit of listening critically to announcers and take notice of their "lapses" in proper diction and articulation.

WORD	CORRECT	INCORRECT
for	should sound like "door"	fur
you're	should sound like "door"	yer
today	too-day	tah-day
to	too	ta
get	should sound like "net"	git
tomorrow	too-morrow	tah-morrow
our	should sound like "sour"	are
ten	should sound like "pen	tin
listening	lis-en-ing	lis-ning
soft drink	pronounce the "t"	sof-drink
tonight	too-night	tah-night
been	should sound like "pen"	bin
getting	should sound like "wetting"	gitting
insurance	in-shur-ance	in-shore-ance
many	should sound like "plenty"	mini
delicious	dee-licious	dah-licious

WORD	CORRECT	INCORRECT
can	should sound like "can"	kin
their	should sound like "air"	thur
forty	pronounce the "t"	fordy
twenty	twen-tee	twunny
Friday	Fri-day	Fri-dee
just	should sound like "rust"	jist
interstate	pronounce the "t"	inner-state
than	should sound like "ran"	then
government	pronounce the "n"	gover-ment
anytime	annie-time	ini-time
plenty	pronounce the "t"	plenny
remember	ree-mem-ber	ree-mim-ber
hundred	hun-dred	hunnerd
police	po-lice	pah-lice
attend	should sound like "pend"	attind
forget	for-get	fur-git
thirty	pronounce the "t"	thurdy
because	should sound like "applause"	be-cuz
W	dubble-yoo	dubb-ya
theatre	thee'-ah-ter	thee-ay'-ter
tender	should sound like "pen"	tinder
candidate	can-did-ate	canna-dit
program	pro-gram	pro-grum
are	should sound like "bar"	er
nuclear	noo-clee-ar	noo-cue-ler
February	Feb-roo-ary	Feb-oo-ary
library	ly-brary	ly-berry
strength	let the "g" ring	strenth
realty	ree-al-tee	reel-a-tee
escape	es-cape	ex-cape
espresso	es-presso	ex-presso
coupon	koo-pon	kew-pon
catch	cahtch	ketch

WORD	CORRECT	INCORRECT
veterinarian	vet-er-in-air-ian	vet-trin-air-ian
arctic	ark-tik	ar-tic
potato	pronounce the "t's"	potado
recognize	rec-og-nize	rec-o-nize
boundary	bound-ah-ree	bound-ree
chocolate	choc-oh-lit	choc-lit
remember	ree-mem-ber	rah-mem-ber
diamond	di-ah-mond	di-mond
battery	bat-er-ee	bat-tree
butter	but-ter	bud-der
picture	pik-ture	pitch-er
✷jewelry	jew-el-ree	√jew-lar-ee or √jewl-ree
prevent	pree-vent	pruh-vent or per-vent
produce	proh-duce	pruh-duce or per-duce

*Special pronunciation notes:

Be careful not to over-enunciate. Your read will sound stilted and phony!

Be sure to give the ending "ing" its full value. Avoid saying goin', doin', or runnin' unless the script is specifically written that way!

When in doubt as to how to say the word "the" as thee or thuh, use what is most conversational. When the next word begins with a vowel, use thee. Otherwise, stick with thuh.
    Example: "Please pass me thee apple".
    "Please pass me thuh pear".

When using "a" in a sentence, it is more conversational and natural to say it as "uh" rather than "ay." For example, it sounds better to say "it's been uh real pleasure" rather than "it's been ay real pleasure." It will always sound like your reading, not speaking, when you say "ay."

The list could go on endlessly, but you get the idea. Watch your pronunciation and diction! Practice on tape those words that continue to cause you problems.

❻

Commercial Copy Interpretation

COMMERCIAL COPY INTERPRETATION

As a professional voice talent, it is your job to interpret the copy in order to deliver the proper style of read. From the moment you are handed your copy, you should be mentally analyzing a number of things:

1. What is the product or service I am selling?
2. Who is my target audience?
3. Who is the competition?
4. How can one benefit from the product/service?
5 How can I best sell that product using my voice?
6. Where is the disclaimer?

Let's take a look at the first question. What product is the spot trying to sell? This may determine the type of emotion and energy you'll want to use. You will give a much more subdued read to promote annual mammograms than you will to promote a new sports car on the market. You will be much more hyped talking about a new video game than you will about fungus medicine. Understand the product or service and let that initially determine your mood of delivery. Another strong point to remember is the *product* is the star of the spot, not you! It's a humbling fact of life, but it's true.

The second question relates to your target audience. Who is going to buy this product? Are you speaking to 15-year old boys or 60-year old women? Each calls for a very different delivery! That 15-year old couldn't care less about a new hair color that covers gray...nor does Grandma care about Clearasil. It is your job to relate appropriately to your target. You speak differently to different audiences about different products.

You need to respect your listener, understand the product, and communicate in a believable manner. Consumers are more sophisticated than ever, and will detect insincerity or unrealistic promises. Your delivery needs to carry credibility, sincerity, and conviction. Granted, you usually don't have control over content, but you do control how it is communicated! Consider age, sex, income, education, lifestyle, and location.

Establishing the identity of the competition can assist in your mental interpretation of the copy. Who or what are you going up against? From there you can determine the unique selling factor you will be emphasizing in your read. For example, if you are doing a spot for Volvo, your unique selling factor would probably be safety. Every product likes to boast one particular feature or image. You need to get that across through your inflection and emotion in the read.

Next, how is one going to benefit from this product or service? This is where emotion comes into the picture. Emotion is the big motivator. Emotion provokes someone to buy. You get someone charged up about how a product will benefit them, and it's sold! It is now your job to convince your target that the product will somehow improve the quality of their life in some way. You must convince them they either need or want that product. Benefits to the consumer could include increased attractiveness and confidence, less out-of-pocket spending, more leisure time, increased prestige or image, greater sex appeal, increased ease of a laborious or boring chore, or improved health. You need to relay the message to your listener in a way that creates a reason he or she will be better off simply by buying that product or service. You need to create a demand. If you are unfamiliar with the product or service, do not hesitate to ask! The more you know about a product, the easier it is to relay that information to your audience in a believable manner.

You then need to determine how to best sell that product using just your voice. You are now the link between the product and the consumer. It is up to you to convey the message and emotion that will provoke sales. Generally the voice talent doesn't have a whole lot of say in the content of the finished copy, so you need to do the very best you can with what you have been given to work.

Finally, you need to identify the disclaimer. By law, many spots have to include disclaimers in their advertising. These are little legal "qualifiers" not unlike the fine print you will find at the bottom of a contract. The most common type of ad in which you will always hear a disclaimer is an automobile ad. After they tout the benefits of leasing, there will be all sorts of details and terms in a hushed and rushed voice. These are *not* selling points, and should not be read as such. You do not want to draw attention to them, so you therefore under-emphasize these disclaimers in your read.

There is a formula in commercial copywriting and marketing referred to as AIDA that has proven to be effective. Let's take a look at it.

AIDA:

A: Attention

The first few seconds of a spot are critical in grabbing your listener's attention. If you do not capture it then, you probably will not get it at all. Attention is not always attained with bells and whistles, but with words and the way they are read. It has got to be interesting and it has got to make the listener want to hear more. These initial words intended to gain attention are called the "hook" and must be read with importance.

I: Interest

Your inflections and emotions must make the listener want to hear more about the benefits of a product, or even the disadvantages of *not* having it. You must determine the most interesting or important benefit of a product and then relay that through your read. Become aware of what makes people react. If you are excited, you will excite your listener.

D: Desire

Now you have to make them want it. This is where the emotional appeal comes into play. Place yourself in your listener's shoes, and deliver in a way that would sell *you* on the product. If you generate your own desire, it comes across through your performance.

A: Action

This is the moment you tell your listener where to go and how to obtain the product or service. This is the moment you save the day and give them a solution to their needs. You usually need to express urgency...through your words, inflections, energy, and excitement. Many spots end with a "stinger," similar to a hook in that it regenerates their interest and makes the product memorable. This is your last chance in the spot to leave your indelible mark on their memory.

By now, you should have a pretty good grasp on what is expected of you as a hired voiceover talent. You have worked on your style, inflection, pacing, diction and delivery. Why not take some time and put yourself to the test. Chapter 15 contains six copy samples for your personal practice. Cassette #3 is specifically for this purpose. Use a stopwatch or a second hand on a clock to check yourself for timing. Listen back and give yourself some honest critique. Practice and practice until you are satisfied with your timing, pacing, and delivery. Do *you* think it's good enough to put on the air?

7

Voiceover Jargon

VOICEOVER JARGON

As with any profession, there are terms and phrases that are unique to that field. Just so you don't look ignorant or respond in a "dumb or dumber" manner, let's review the common terminology you will hear in the recording studio.

The *COPY* is the written script for the commercial advertisement.

You may hear the copy being described as *FAT* or *HEAVY*, *THIN* or *LIGHT*. It is merely an assessment of the quantity of words in the ad. Fat or heavy copy indicates that there is a lot to read in the designated time. Either you will need to really hustle along in your read, or they will need to take out some of the words. In contrast, thin or light copy means either a slow delivery on your part, or they will have to add more words for you to read.

You have heard the term *DISCLAIMER*. Automobile spots tend to have the most. It refers to those little legal statements that are required by law to accompany a given advertising statement. In other words, it is the "fine print" of the spoken language. As the talent, all you need to do is recognize them and then downplay them in your read. Disclaimers are *not* selling points and should be treated accordingly.

A *SPOT* is simply another term for the commercial or advertisement.

Frequently your voice will be recorded over what is called a **MUSIC BED**. Recording studios always have a music library, which is a collection of CD's just loaded with all kinds of music. Produced music beds have no singing vocals on them. They are designed to be played under spoken words. The producer and client will go through the CD's and select the music that seems to best fit the style and energy level of the spot. The music is recorded onto a track and is then played back through your headphones as you record. In this situation, you are recording *over* a music bed. In other situations, you may record your voice alone, or dry, and the music will be added later in post-production. The client may even bring in a taped jingle or music bed they use with all their commercials.

A **JINGLE** is a pre-recorded music bed with singing. It may have only 5 or 10 seconds of singing, and the rest is filled in with your voiceover. The singing could be at the beginning, in the middle or at the end. You never talk over the singing vocals! If there is singing at the beginning *and* at the end, it is called a **DONUT**. In that case, your voiceover must be timed perfectly to fit within the singing.

The **MIKE** is an abbreviated term for the microphone.

Your mike may have a **WIND SCREEN** positioned in front of it. This is a small, thin circular screen mounted directly between your mouth and the microphone to help reduce unwanted mouth noises and pops. Many times you will simply see a foam cover or "sock" placed directly over the end of the mike.

POPS, as long as we are talking about them, are those obnoxious pops you hear when you force air directly into the mike when pronouncing hard letters like p, t, or k. You can hear those pops in your headphones during your read. If you're recording, you may as well stop there and do a retake, because pops are unacceptable for the finished product. If you are not recording but just practicing for timing, then carry on! Work on softening your pronunciation of words with p's in them and speak diagonally across the mike rather than directly into the end of it. Some brands of mikes are more sensitive to pops than others.

HEADPHONES are self-explanatory, and can also be referred to as earphones or, in slang...phones or cans. Headphones allow you to hear your own voice as well as other voices, music beds and sound effects. They also enable you to communicate with your director, who is usually in another room. Headphones are provided by the studio or you can travel with your own. This may be preferable if this voiceover stuff becomes a regular gig. You then have control over the brand, fit, comfort, sound quality and cleanliness. Recording studios have no problem with you using your own phones.

When everyone is getting situated and set up, your engineer will tell you through your headphones, "Give me a *LEVEL*." At that point, you begin reading your script exactly the way you will read it when you begin recording...the same volume and the same distance from the mike. He is adjusting your volume levels in preparation to record. After your levels are set, be sure not to move around and alter your mouth-to-mike distance and placement. By the way, when asked for a level, don't just say "test, one, two." Your engineer not only needs more to work with, he needs to hear how you will read the spot. The actual copy will generate more projection in your voice than "test, one, two."

As you are standing at the mike ready to give a read, you may hear your director say "*ROLLING!*" He is telling you that he is now ready to record and it is your cue to begin your slate, count-in, then your read.

If your director wants a *SLATE*, then before you begin reading your copy, state the name of the spot and which "take" you are doing. For example, "Folger's Coffee, take 3." This aids in the editing process later. The producers are taking notes as to which read they like the best, and it is easier for them to identify the right take on the tape if it is slated.

It is customary to give your producer a *COUNT-IN*. Many times this is incorporated into your slate. This is particularly helpful to the engineer if he is trying to get an exact time on your read. It indicates to him/her when to begin the timing. You would say into the mike, for example, "Take 2 in three, two, one..." Then in the same tempo and pacing, begin your first word of the spot. It is done just as a bandleader would conduct his musicians to begin playing simultaneously.

A *TAKE* is a run-through of the spot. You may hear something like "Let's do another take, only this time with more energy"...or "That was good. Let's do a take for safety." Your director is simply telling you to do it again.

If you are directed to do another take for *SAFETY*, it means the producer or client is satisfied with what you have done. However, unexpected problems may arise in post-production and it is always wise to have another good version for backup. It sure beats being called back into the studio for a redo!

You will hear the word *CUT* used in several different ways. Your director may tell you to cut something out of your copy. In other words, delete it from your next take. You may be in the middle of a read and hear your director say "cut" in your headphones. You simply stop reading and wait for further direction.

Let's say you have gotten through most of your commercial and either you make a mistake or the director wants to make a change in the copy. Your engineer may tell you "Let's do a *PUNCH-IN* at the end of the previous sentence." This is a very convenient process, saving you from having to go back and start from the beginning. He will play back in your headphones the part you have already recorded, then you jump back in live at the point it needs to be recorded over.

If you have done a totally awesome job on your last take, it is referred to as a *KEEPER*. You may be asked to do another take for safety purposes, but they will keep the read you just did.

If they do not need another take for safety, you will hear that magical phrase "That's a *WRAP!*" It means you can pack up and head for the beach.

The client or director will always need copies of the finished commercial. These copies are referred to as *DUBS*. For example, if the spot is going to be played on four radio stations, then four dubs, or copies of the spots, will need to be produced.

The *MIXING CONSOLE* or *MIXING BOARD* is that huge piece of equipment with a trillion or so buttons on it. Don't freak...you don't have to touch it! This is where all the recording and mixing is done by the sound engineer.

The *MIX* is the final balance of all the sound elements in the spot. You may have music, voices, and sound effects that comprise the finished product. The level of each element is adjusted to a well-balanced blend.

You will hear your engineer make reference to the various *TRACKS*. Recording studios are multi-track, meaning numerous different sounds can be recorded on each different track. That way, the varying elements such as voices, music and sound effects can all be controlled independently of each other. Most studios are 8-track, 16-track, 24-track or 48-track. More tracks mean more available sources of audio.

Most studios are now using *DIGITAL RECORDING AND EDITING.* This incorporates the use of computers with recording and editing software programs. The quality of sound and the ease of editing have been greatly improved with the use of computers. It is a huge improvement over tape and reel-to-reel machines, and the old "splicing and editing" routine with a wax pencil, razor blade and editing tape. Although tape is still very widely used, it is quickly becoming obsolete.

ABBREVIATIONS THAT APPEAR ON COPY:

VO:	Voiceover
MX:	Music
ANNCR:	The announcer's part in the script
M:	The male's lines in a script
F:	The female's lines in a script
SFX:	Sound effects that will be integrated into the finished recording

8

Making Your Demo Tape

MAKING YOUR DEMO TAPE

Your demo tape is your calling card. It is your identity and distinction in the business. It is your talent showcase. It is the tool that generates employment. That 50-cent item can reap thousands of dollars for your bank account. Therefore, it is the single most important aspect of your business. Your demo tape will make or break your career in voiceovers.

YOUR MISSION: TO CREATE A GREAT DEMO TAPE AND PLACE IT DIRECTLY IN THE HANDS OF ANYONE AND EVERYONE WHO CAN GET YOU A VOICEOVER JOB.

Your demo has to be nothing less than fabulous. It has to have clout. It has to have impact from start to finish. It has to have excitement, enticement, dimension, diversity, energy, and entertainment value. Most of the time you get voice work directly from your demo tape, not an audition.

There are a lot of details involved in creating your demo tape in a professional manner, so I'll run down the list for you. Take note of these and apply them carefully when making your tape. There could be some minor variations depending on your market size, but a great tape is a great tape...and a great tape gets you work.

POINTERS FOR A GREAT VOICEOVER DEMO TAPE

- Find access to *professional equipment*. Your tape must be high quality to compete with others. Your voice must be clear and concise, pleasant to listen to and easy to understand. Under no circumstances should you even *think* of using a home cassette recorder! You need a professional microphone and professional recording and duplication facilities. The judgement process of your tape begins within the first 4 to 5 seconds, and a muffled tape will get a very muffled response...and probably be shut off and the cassette recycled.

- Use *high quality cassettes*. Spring for that extra nickel when purchasing your tapes. Poor quality tapes tend to muffle the clear, crisp high frequencies that add brilliance to your audio. Good quality cassettes display the best quality voice audio. This is *not* an area where you should cut costs! Your tapes should be bought in bulk from an audio supply dealership in total lengths of 6 to 10 minutes. That gives you 3 to 5 minutes per side. An excellent source for mail order recording supplies is Tapes Unlimited at 800-276-6175.

- The *ideal length* of the demo tape that you are shooting for is 2 minutes. You want to showcase as much range of talent as possible in that time frame.

- You will use only about 10 or 15 seconds for each spot, so there is more opportunity than you may think when looking at only 2 minutes. I doubt anyone would spend more time listening to a demo anyway, even if they really liked it. Keep in mind that after the first 5 seconds they already know if you may be right or wrong for the job!

- Choose *copy that stimulates listening and enhances your talent.* Use national spots versus local spots. It gives you a "bigger" image. A spot for Toyota is far more impressive than a spot for Wally's Swap Shop. Your demo does not have to be a "resume" of what you have *done,* but rather what you are *capable* of doing. In other words, it is an audible demonstration of your abilities, not accomplishments. You are not misrepresenting yourself by using commercials you have not actually been hired to do.

- The best way to *get the best copy* is to record some commercials from your television and then transcribe them onto paper. You will only be using the first 10 or 15 seconds of the commercial, so it is quick and simple. Try to avoid the very well-known spots, but rather use those that are less-known, well-written and exciting. Humor also goes a long way toward entertaining your listener. Accumulate about 8 to 10 commercials.

- When selecting your material, use caution to choose only those *spots that are appropriate for your voice and abilities.* You want to display diversity and range of talent, but you do not want to show what you *can't* do well! Make sure you have chosen the widest range possible in style, pacing and intensity. Also choose a wide range of products.

- Another consideration is your *voice age range.* Listen to your voice on tape compared to others. Determine what age range you have the ability to cover and chose your material accordingly. If you have a young, high-pitched voice, you will sound rather unconvincing in a Depends spot. If you have an older, deep male voice, stay away from doing Pampers. Use good judgement in choosing good material. Gear your choices toward your voice age range, while at the same time showing both extremes of your range spectrum.

- You will want to make *tasteful use of music and sound effects* in your spot, just like on radio and television. However, use caution not to let those elements drown you out. Keep the music at "enhancement" levels and sound effects to a minimum. It is also important to keep your voice as natural as possible without a lot of fancy effects. Avoid lots of echo and reverb so the prospective client can hear what you *really* sound like.

- *Do not use same-sex two-voicers.* If you are thinking of including a spot that was recorded with another talent of the same sex as you, forget it! What happens if the client likes the other voice more than yours? Do not waste your valuable demo time advertising another talent. It is okay to use a voice of the opposite sex, but only if it enhances and showcases yours. If the other voice is doing all the talking, you may as well be *their* agent, not your own! The best policy is to stick with your own voice.

- If you are a talented actor and have some really good *character voices* up your sleeve, by all means showcase them. Use original characters that are yours alone. Do not steal voices! If you have a good character, find a spot for which it works. If you cannot find an appropriate spot for that character, you are better off leaving it out. Also, if your characters are not so good or you know they need work, don't use them! Any time you step outside your talent range, it detracts from what you *can* do.

- After you have voiced and produced your spots, review them carefully, and preferably with the opinion of another professional ear. Pick your strongest spot and place it first in the line-up. S*tart strong*! If the client does not like what he hears from the start, he will not continue to listen. Then, place the spots in a sequence that enhances the range of your talent. Vary the pacing, energy, and the products.

- When producing the finished product, *place your spots right up against each other* to keep the flow fast-paced and moving forward. Avoid fade-outs and fade-ins from spot to spot. That creates a very fragmented sound that becomes uncomfortable to the listener. Fade-outs and fade-ins also detract from the overall momentum of your tape.

- Use *different demo tapes for different voiceover jobs*. If you are trying to land a job voicing a documentary for Motorola, the client will not want to endure peanut butter commercials and mouse characters to hear what your speaking voice sounds like. Develop one tape specifically for commercials, one for industrials, and one for characters. If you only have one or two characters, however, you can incorporate them into your commercial demo. Keep the industrial or corporate demo separate. Here are a few options. You could have a commercial demo on side one of the tape and an industrial demo on side two. If you choose this method, make sure the cassettes are short in length and clearly labeled. If you do have a good family of characters, you can make three separate tapes and then package them together. This way the client can save time by going directly to what he or she needs to hear for that particular job. It creates a nice little showcase or platform in which to show off each facet of your great talent.

- *Keep your demo current.* Get yourself into the studio from time to time to update your demo. The longer you are in the business, the better you will get. You always want to show off your best work, and that is usually the most recent work.

POINTERS FOR PACKAGING YOUR DEMO TAPE

You've heard the old adage...you can only make a first impression once. How true it is. You want your first impression to have impact and influence. You want your prospective client to climb fences to get your voice on his next job. You want your client to accept no other than the best, and that is *you*. Okay, so much for dreaming, but you certainly do not want your tape to land up in the trash, or recycled for other purposes! I have outlined a few points for you to consider when packaging that demo you have spent so much time putting together.

* *Label your cassettes properly and professionally.* Again, your demo is your calling card. You need to use the same professionalism in labeling as you would in designing your business card. Your labels should be typed or printed. If you have a home computer, labeling is an easy task. Most desktop publishing programs have standard cassette label templates that are very user-friendly. Standard Avery labels, or labels ordered from a mail-order audio supply source will work nicely. Labels can be ordered in a variety of colors, so choose something that coordinates with your chosen color scheme.

- The *information* you put on your cassette label is very important. Of course, your name is good for starters. If you have created different tapes for different jobs, you will want to identify which demo it is for. For example, you may have three different labels that read "Commercial Demo," "Industrial Demo," and "Character Demo." It is also a courtesy to include the length of the demo. It is less threatening to the listener if they know what they are in for. If your tape is labeled 2:00, they know at the end of two minutes, it is done. They do not have to keep the tape rolling to see if there is anything else there. Most importantly, your phone number should appear somewhere on the label. It is very easy for a cassette to become separated from its case. What if the client absolutely loves your tape, but cannot find the business card that came with it and therefore will never know how to contact you? That's a lousy way to lose a job! Here are a couple of examples of good labeling:

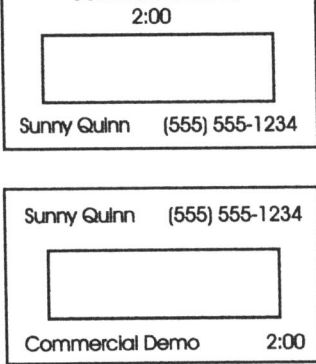

- If you have a single cassette, you may insert your business card in the case or have an *insert label* printed. If you go with the insert, include all the information again, but also have your name printed in bold lettering on the spine of the cassette case.

- If you have *multiple cassettes*, you will be using a molded, plastic book-type case that holds the cassettes without the individual cases. With the help of a desktop publishing program or your professional printer, you can design an attractive cover. Again, the spine label should not be ignored! Use color to your advantage, but don't go too crazy. Keep it simple and bold.

- When having your tapes duplicated, use a *real-time duplication* process. High-speed duplication tends to diminish the high-end frequencies that add clarity and sharpness to your audio. These tapes are short anyway, so it is well worth the extra time to keep the quality at its absolute best.

- After you have your recorded cassettes, take the time to *pop out the tabs* on the spine of the cassette rendering it impossible to record over without taping up the tab gaps. It is too easy to hit the record button when listening back. Or someone might need a cassette and grab whatever is around. In an unfortunate circumstance, it could be your demo tape. If they cannot record on it without first taping up those safety gaps, they might just find themselves another cassette.

- The subject of *photographs* comes up frequently. Should you or should you not include a head shot in your demo package? Opinions differ, as photos can definitely work for or against you. For example, suppose a client is looking for a witch voice for a Halloween campaign. Then they see a photo of a gorgeous young blond woman on the cover of your demo package. They will assume from your picture that you cannot possibly be capable of portraying an ugly old witch! Maybe they want a teenage-sounding female. They see from your photo that you are close to 50. Well, guess what? Your voice could have an outstanding 18-year old sound, but you will never get the chance to prove it. Maybe the client needs a big boomy male megavoice, and they see from your picture that you're a scrawny little 100-pound weakling with a pocket protector and gets sand kicked in his face at the beach. It is natural to typecast someone from their photo and therefore not even bother to listen to the tape. If you omit your picture, they can judge only from their imagination and that can work to your advantage. Now let's toss the coin. Perhaps the client is looking for an on-camera talent as well as a voice talent. You could very easily nail down the job if they like what they see from your photo. The choice of including a photo has to be left up to you. I do happen to have a very small black and white head shot on the back cover of my demo package, which is a book-type multi-cassette case. I think I have fared well with the inclusion of my photo, but will I ever know if I have *lost* any work because of it? Nope. Understand that it's a very individual choice that is now yours.

* Always keep in mind that the *appearance of your finished product* reflects your professionalism. It speaks volumes about how you feel about yourself and your abilities. If a prospective client receives a sloppy demo, it is only natural to assume that your work ethics are also sloppy. If your demo is sharp they will assume that you, too, are one sharp cookie.

9

Finding The Jobs

FINDING THE JOBS

The imagination is a wonderful thing. If there was ever a time to put it to use, it is now. Even after years in the business, I still trip over new ideas and new ways to put the ol' voice to work. For now, though, let's start with the obvious and you can take it from there depending on your market and your ambition.

Arm yourself with the latest phone books from all your surrounding towns or counties from as far away as you are willing to drive for a voiceover job. You will also need a stack of 3x5 index cards. There are several different headings you will want to check.

Begin with *Video Production Services*. This is a potential gold mine of voice work! You will want to call each studio and have a separate index card for each one. On the card, jot down the name of the studio, the address, and phone number. After you speak with the studio you will add such information as the name of the production director, the name of the secretary or receptionist, the specialty of that particular studio, and if you decided to send them a demo package. Some studios specialize in videotaping weddings and really have no use for voiceover talent. Make a note of that on the index card for future reference and do not waste your money sending them a demo.

Find the studios that do creative video work requiring the talents of a voiceover artist. Most production directors are grateful to add new voices to their talent bank, providing they like what they hear. If you and the director decide that it is in everyone's best interest for you to send or drop off a demo package, do so promptly! If you mail it, check back in a few days to make sure he or she received it, then again a few days after that to see if he has had the time to listen to it. If so, feel free to ask for feedback. If he hasn't, don't pressure him! Just tell him you will check back again in another few days to see if yours is a voice he may be able to utilize in the future. Every time you have a communication with that studio, make a note of the date and the nature of your communication on the index card. You will then be able to refer back to it and be current with what has transpired.

I mentioned adding the name of the secretary or receptionist to the index card. In most offices, the receptionist is the "keeper of the gate." Befriend this person! She or he largely dictates who gets through to the boss. If you call and mention her by name, you will have instantly made points! She will remember you for the simple reason you remembered her. It works!

The next heading you should check out is *Recording Studios*. This is your other major source of work. Run through the same procedure as with video studios. Again, most studios will be receptive to a new talent and will welcome your demo tape. You may not get work from these new sources, but you will usually be treated kindly. There have been cases when it has been more than two years from the time a studio received a demo to the time they called me in for a job. Some studios offer work only once or twice a year. Others call 2 or 3 times a week. You never know initially which ones will pan out. You need to contact all of them and then remind them of your existence and availability from time to time.

Another source to check out is your local cable stations, usually listed under *Television-Cable & Satellite*. Most cable stations have in-house production facilities. There is an enormous amount of steady work at the local companies. Some cable companies even have a tourist information channel, which is predominately voiced over. They may feature locally-produced programming offering even more voiceover opportunities. In addition, they need to sell advertising to stay in business, and someone is hired to voice their commercials. Most cable companies will also need someone to record their message-on-hold and voice mail. You may even find opportunities to do on-camera work if you are so inclined! Keep in mind cable companies are notorious for being low payers, but it is usually fairly steady work. Do not forget to check out your "local access" station, too. This is definitely not a source to be overlooked.

Some *Television Stations* have their own in-house production facilities. You may want to call the production departments of the stations in your area and check. If they do produce commercials in-house, by all means provide them with a demo package! They are always looking for fresh voices.

While video production, recording studios and cable TV stations will be your prime sources of contacts and jobs, do not limit yourself there! Make calls to *Advertising & Marketing Agencies.* Many times they book the talent themselves. Ask how much broadcast advertising they place in relation to print. If it is a significant percentage, say 20% or more, it could be beneficial to send them a demo. The drawback is there are usually numerous agents within the company and your tape would only be reaching one. If it is a small agency or even a one-man agency, that will work. If it is a large agency, you need to make all the agents aware of your work without stepping on toes. Most successful advertising agency contacts can be discovered at the actual recording sessions. You could be booked by the studio and then meet the agent at the session. If they like you, they will request to have you back for future sessions.

Telephone Communications Services may offer a service that sets up businesses with message-on-hold. For example, when you call your car dealership and they put you on hold, a recorded voice is explaining the value the dealership places on its customers, hours of business, types of warranties offered on their new and used cars, etc. This way there is no "down time" when you are on hold. You are still receiving information about that dealership while you are waiting for your party to pick up. This is a great source of voiceover work! You can even create your own message-on-hold demo tapes and market them yourself!

Ever call your local *Movie Theatres*? Again, a recorded voice runs down all the titles and times of that week's movies. What if you approached them with a demo and sold them on the idea of having it professionally produced and updated each week? Many theatres operate on very tight budgets and will tell you the popcorn girl records them. Again, you get what you pay for and maybe the theatre manager will eventually come to realize that and hire you.

Now we start in with the imagination thing. How about *Travel Agencies* that want to put together a vacation resort promotional package? Also check with public relations officials of towns, cities, and counties. I have done numerous "travelogues" on resorts and towns. *Departments of Leisure Services, Parks and Recreation Departments* and/or the city's *Chamber of Commerce* have opportunities each year to submit documentaries on their town in national competitions. *Tourist Development Councils* also do similar promotional videos. If any of these agencies use outside studios to produce their videos, find out who they use.

There are companies that work closely with *Attorneys at Law* that specialize in what is known as "visual evidence." These businesses videotape victims and witnesses involved in lawsuits and crimes. A good portion of these tapes needs narration, and there may be a company similar to this in your area.

Check with Human Resources or Public Relations at *Hospitals or medical complexes.* They oversee the production of hospitality videos, orientation videos, instructional videos, advertisements, message-on-hold, and voice menus. They will sometimes hire talent from within their own resources rather than an outside studio. If they do use an outside studio, they will probably be more than happy to share that information with you.

The question of whether to submit your demo package to *Talent Agencies* is a tough one. There are numerous disreputable agencies cropping up all the time, and I do not want to guide you down a destructive path. You need to use care, common sense, discretion, and good judgement concerning talent agencies. For some, they work well. I know others who have gotten into regrettable situations. Outside of large cities, agents generally don't even specialize in this type of talent booking and you could probably do just fine without them.

After you have established yourself in the biz, you may want to expand your horizons. If you have the talent for the big work, you may want to reach into areas outside your own. There are many publications and source directories of studios across the country, and an especially good one is *Shoot*. This gives names, addresses, phone numbers, and specialty details for studios all over the country and breaks them down into different categories. It covers everything from motion picture animation studios to commercial production houses to advertising agencies. It will run you about fifty bucks, and can be acquired at Shoot, 1515 Broadway, New York, New York 10036, or call (212) 764-7300.

In summary, take mental note of every voice you hear. Somewhere, somehow that voice was recorded and someone got paid for it! Think of the logical places they would produce that type of work, ask around, and make yourself known and available. Network, network, network...and *always* have business cards and demo tapes on you!

⑩

Establishing Contacts & Follow-up

ESTABLISHING CONTACTS

I mentioned previously to fill out an index card for each job lead. Every time you have some sort of contact with that company, make note of it on the card. Keep track of names, titles, proper spellings, specialty work, and any miscellaneous information they give you. If you speak with someone on the phone or stop by, or even do a recording job for them, note it. Once you get busy it is tough keeping track of all those contacts. It is easy to let months go by without making any contact with a potential employer. Keep in mind they may not have any work for you when you first contact them and if months go by before something comes up, they could have forgotten all about you by then. It is important to remind them on a regular basis that you are ready, willing and able to do a voiceover job.

Once you have made your initial call and you both decide it would be beneficial for you to send a demo tape, send it out that day or the next. Do not wait! If they have just spoken with you on the phone, they will be more inclined to give it a listen when it arrives. Then give a follow-up call about 3 or 4 business days later just to be certain that it was received. They will usually respond with a yes and continue to mention if they have had the opportunity to listen to it or not. If not, assure them that it's okay, you were just checking in to see if it was received. Tell him you will check back after a few days to get his feedback and to see if you might be a voice they could use in the future. Then call back!

Give him another 3 to 4 days and call again before it slips his mind. If he has had a chance to listen to the tape, ask for his opinion and take it from there.

Once you are assured the studio has your demo and the director has heard your tape, you still may not hear from them. Most likely they are still assigning their voiceovers to their regular talent who has been working with them all along, or maybe it is a slow time and there just isn't any voice work at the moment. Maybe they are working on a long-term project and haven't taken on any new stuff, or maybe they were just being nice and they really do not like your voice work! In some situations, you will never really know. In others, you will.

Have postcards printed similar in design to your business card. Go through your index cards and find the studios that you have not had contact with in 4 to 6 weeks. On the back of the postcards, hand write a brief, personal note simply reminding them that you exist and are still available. There are those lucky times when your card may arrive the same day they sign on a new client and guess who comes to mind first? Many jobs come down to pure luck. They may have received a reminder card at just the right moment or you happen to be there when another job came in the door. It doesn't matter how you get it, just as long as you get it!

The reminder postcards are a friendly and non-intrusive way to keep in touch. You are not pulling the producer away from his work to respond but rather nudging his memory that you are available. It keeps you in the forefront of his mind. It signals to him that you are a business professional. This is your livelihood and you take it seriously. After you send out your reminder postcards, note it on your index cards!

CONTACT FOLLOW-UP

Now that you have established all these great sources for potential voice work, you need to reinforce and nurture these new relationships. If you let them fall by the wayside, your career will do the same. Here are some major points to keep in mind:

- Determine who the appropriate contact person is at each location and exactly who should receive the tape.

- At the end of your initial conversation with that person, ask permission to call back. This clears the way for a follow-up call.

- Learn the names and positions of the support staff. They appreciate it and will think highly of you in return.

- Make friends with the "gate-keepers." The secretaries and receptionists often determine who gets through to the producer and who does not. Also many receptionists move up through the ranks and could even become the next casting director of that studio!

- Every contact is critical. People move around and people get promoted. You never know who may pick up that phone at the new recording studio in town. Treat people well and keep your reputation impeccable.

- Time your follow-up calls carefully. Most busy people do not want your phone call at 9:00 Monday morning or 5:00 Friday afternoon. The best days are Tuesday, Wednesday or Thursday. The best hours to call are between 10 a.m. and noon, and 2 to 4 p.m.

- Have consideration for what the person at the other end of line may be doing when you call. If he or she sounds hurried or hassled, they probably are. Ask if it would be better that you call another time. They will remember your thoughtfulness and appreciate it. Ask when a good time might be and with that response, you will be getting his permission to call again.

- If he tells you to call back at a certain time or on a certain day, do it! When you do call, remind him that he told you to call at this time. He will be far more receptive to speaking with you if you made it look like he is the one who asked you to call.

- During the course of your conversation, ask questions. Encourage two-way dialogue to keep him or her interested and focused. Evoking responses also goes a long way in keeping your conversation memorable.

- Always ask if there may be something coming up that your voice would be suitable for. Your goal is to keep your name foremost in his or her mind.

- Persistence in follow-up contact will usually turn into success in landing a job. Your name will be familiar and they will probably want to reward you for all your tireless efforts!

- Be available and quickly accessible. They won't chase you for long. Stay in touch with your answering system and return calls promptly.

- Be organized. This business can get pretty crazy when you consider that with each job you have a different boss. Names, jobs, clients, billing, and studios can become a big blur if not kept straight from the beginning. Take notes, keep files, and stay current in your paperwork.

- Always be happy, friendly and positive. People like to work with happy people. If they enjoy your company they will very likely call you back for more. Besides, you'll enjoy life more, too.

①①

Behind Studio Doors

BEHIND STUDIO DOORS

In the beginning of your exciting new career, the recording studio can be a very intimidating environment. You will discover that the studio takes on many faces. In your travels from studio to studio you will probably see everything from converted garages or closets to state-of-the-art digital super-suites! Most studios will fall somewhere in between. Keep in mind there is only one goal, regardless of the set-up of the physical plant, and that is to achieve the best quality voice work for that particular job. Your job remains the same whether you are in Freddy's garage or Mr. Rockefeller's Super Duper Space Age Sound Stage. Stay focused and do not allow yourself to be distracted by your surroundings.

STUDIO ETIQUETTE

WHAT TO BRING WITH YOU

Come prepared! Just like you would with any job, you take what you need to get the job done. You do not want to get into a situation where you have to mooch off your boss! The tools of the trade are few, but important.

Bring your *voice* for starters...in good health. If you have a cold or a case of laryngitis, call your studio well ahead of time and see if you can set up another time to record. They hired you for your voice and expect it to be in top form.

Bring your *headphones* if you so choose. This is optional, as most studios will provide them for you. However, they have no problem with you using your own if you prefer. Simply plug them in where the existing ones are and replace them when you are through.

Bring a *pen or pencil* for editing your copy. Invariably changes will need to be made and you won't have to go begging and searching for a writing utensil if you pack your own. I found those pens on a string to wear around your neck are great. I take them off while recording so they don't bump into anything, but they are very accessible and convenient.

Bring a *highlighter*. Your client may ask you to emphasize a particular word or phrase and it is easy to remember if you highlight it.

Bring *business cards*. You never know whom you will meet in a recording session. Lots of voice work stems from other voice work. Pass those cards out like candy to prospective clients at the session and other voice talent you work with. The other talent just might be in a situation to recommend a second voice for a future session. Take advantage of your golden opportunity to network.

Bring *demo cassettes*. For reasons mentioned above, it never hurts to slip a cassette of your voice demo into your pocket. The client may have a job coming up and want to play your voice demo for the "decision makers" back at the office. Also be sure that every recording studio you visit has a current cassette of your voice work.

Bring *invoices*. It is a good system to simply leave an invoice at the studio for the work done in that session. Even if they pay you on the spot they will need it for their records. Mailing invoices after the session is okay but you will need to gather the names and addresses before you leave, then actually remember to send the invoice afterward. Plus, if you leave the invoice there you save on postage. Make sure you keep copies of all invoices for your own records.

PROPER ATTIRE
As creative and fun as recording is, the studio is a professional place of business. Studio time is big money and the talent who wastes it probably will not be invited back! You can be your friendly and personable self but keep in mind that you are a professional. You need to dress and behave accordingly. You don't need to get decked out in your Brooks Brothers or Dior suit, but leave the torn and tattered tie-dyed jeans at home! Dress casually, tastefully, and comfortably. Consider who the client is and use your good judgement. Is the client your local weekend swap shop flea market or a major international corporate giant? In the case of the latter, I would expect some executive-type folks to be there and would perhaps take a step up in my clothing selection. Some recording situations take several hours on your feet...so for you gals, high heels could be quite inappropriate, if not excruciatingly painful. Use common sense and be practical!

HYGIENE

Often when you have been hired to record a spot, you do not really know the nature of the spot until you arrive at the studio. You may not even know if it is a single or multi-voice spot. You could end up working with other voice talent and many times in very close quarters! Spare your co-workers and leave the cologne or perfume for your lover. Your cologne could kick off a sneezing fit by one of your co-workers and totally destroy the session! I have seen it happen and it's *not* pretty! Most people do not care to be overwhelmed by the smell of another in such close quarters, especially when breathing and voice are so critical. Gosh, for that reason alone, don't forget your deodorant and mouthwash! While we are being blunt, clean hair goes a long way, too. Those headphones are shared by many!

JEWELRY

When dressing for your recording or audition session, it is wise to leave excess jewelry at home. You are not in the recording studio to "impress by dress" anyway. I have seen a perfectly good recording destroyed by the clanking of a bracelet or neck chain against the microphone or copy stand. Also, earrings are very uncomfortable under headphones! Rings and chokers are fine. It is that dangling stuff that will get you into trouble every time.

DRINKS

As a rule of thumb, fluids do not belong anywhere near that extremely expensive equipment! Forget walking into a recording studio while you finish up your morning cup of coffee. I have seen full cups of coffee loaded with cream and sugar get accidentally dumped into $50,000 mixing boards. For some reason, the owner of that equipment gets very testy...not a good way to kick off a long-term working relationship. Most likely your producer will have no problem with you keeping a closed, spill-proof bottle of drinking water with you...the kind joggers and bikers use. Not all studios have bottled water on hand and you will need it for the longer sessions. Unless anything else is offered to you, stick with that and you will be okay. Be sure to eat before your session so your stomach doesn't decide to get in on the act and growl at you during your takes!

BEHAVE YOURSELF
Okay, so maybe I'm sounding like your mom or teacher, but good behavior is critical! Excess chatter and laughter and clowning around can cost you the next gig. The client is paying dearly for hourly studio time and will not appreciate your wasting his time and money. Don't take this to extremes and be a stuffed shirt either. You have been hired for your talent and personality...just use it appropriately. It's great to have a little fun, but it is business. Listen carefully to your director. Follow that direction to the best of your ability. If you're talking, you're not listening. Also, give your engineer complete and total silence at the end of a take. He will need that space of "dead air" for editing purposes. If you come in directly after your last word with more babbling or a big breath or rustling papers, he ends up with a more difficult editing task. These things may seem trivial and unimportant but it is just

one more element that separates the pros from the amateurs. It is these little things that may influence who they hire as their next voice talent.

SHUT UP OR SPEAK UP

As you gain experience, the choice to shut up or speak up will become obvious to you. Many times the copy is too long or too short or poorly structured. Sometimes you will notice improper English. This can be a touchy subject. Enter...ego. The person who wrote the copy could be sitting right there and become deeply offended if you start remarking about faults in the copy. They want to be the boss and have you read the spot just as they wrote it. In that situation, shut up! At the other end of the spectrum, some clients will see you as a creative authority and will welcome any input you can contribute. They are grateful for your ability to pick up on improper use of a word or improper grammar. In that case, speak up!

There are tactful ways of inquiring as to who wrote the copy. A compliment is always a good way to start. Find an outstanding feature of the spot and comment on it. For example, "This spot describes the product really well. Did you write this?" If he or she did, they will speak right up! If not, they will simply say no, someone back at the office put it together. Bingo! You know right away if you are dealing with the writer. You will develop a sensitivity to this issue as you gain experience in the studio. You will have a big advantage over other talent if you clearly know when to shut up or speak up.

WHEN THE JOB IS DONE...LEAVE!

Some friendly chit chat will transpire when it is a wrap and you head back into the engineering booth. You will double check that the client is happy with your work and that no changes need to be made. You will be writing up your invoice, packing up your headphones and preparing to leave. What you are actually doing is "imprinting" your talent and personality on the client so he or she will remember you and ask for you next time they need a voice! The client will probably stay with the engineer to do post-production and wait for dubs. Before they can get going on that task, you need to leave! Complete your wrap-up duties quickly and efficiently. The more you linger with your idle chatter, the more studio time you waste and the more it will cost the client. Thank the client and the engineer for the opportunity and be on your way.

❶❷

The Audition

THE AUDITION

Ah, the dreaded audition process. Another opportunity for frayed nerves, jittery hands, and a good adrenaline rush. The best way to get over the "audition jitters" is to tackle them head on.

In many larger markets or for very big jobs in smaller markets, the audition is the process that will be utilized by the client to seek out the best person for the job. For the majority of your work, you will simply be called in from your demo tape or your past work at that studio and the audition process will be skipped entirely. Eventually, though, that audition will come your way. You'd best be prepared!

You will hear of job opportunities through a variety of sources. Sometimes an open audition is advertised in the classifieds in your local paper or trade magazine. There may even be a featured article in your newspaper highlighting an upcoming open audition. Open auditions mean they are open to anyone who would like to try out for the job. Expect a "cattle call" and be prepared to wait with lots of hopefuls. Use this time to your advantage. Take a microcassette recorder with you and practice off in a corner. Be friendly, but do not get caught up in waiting room jibber jabber. It is very distracting. These types of auditions bring wanna-be's out of the woodwork from every corner of the city!

There are also closed auditions, or auditions by invitation only. Sources of closed audition notification include a talent agent (if you've been working with one) or the recording studio where the audition is to be held. Frequently the client will rely on the familiarity of the studio director with the available voice talent, so these may come your way after you are more well known in the market. The client may not want to listen to the various demo tapes but would rather hear how you and others will sound reading *their* material. These are usually the high-budget, high-profile jobs...and my favorite type of audition.

The studio will either book a specific time for you or give you a time window to come in to audition, saving you literally *hours*. The competition is less in number, but greater in talent. The talent is personally invited to take part in the closed audition so you can assume they will be pretty good. Do not be afraid or intimidated by the competition! *You* must be good, too, or you would not have been invited. Also, hanging out with other good talent will make *you* better!

You will be informed over the phone about the type of job you are auditioning for. Sometimes they will even provide you with the copy ahead of time. The following is an average scenario for the typical audition. You will arrive at the studio at the designated time. It is best to allow plenty of time for unexpected travel delays! You should carry detailed road maps in your car if you live in a large city or in a town you are not totally familiar with. Arrive five minutes early...not ten...and certainly not *after* your designated time. If you arrive too early, they may still be working with another talent and you will interrupt the session. Arrive too late and you just blew the audition. Not a particularly terrific way to start.

There may be a sign-in sheet in the reception area. Fill it out accordingly...neatly and legibly. Do not forget to bring a pen or pencil with you. That is usually the time you will be handed your copy to look over before you actually go in to record. While you are rehearsing your read, come up with two very different ways of reading the spot. You will want to showcase as much diversity as possible in a very short period of time. You will be instructed from there as to how the session will proceed. They may ask you to slate your name, in which case you simply say "Hi, this is (your name)." Give a pause, then begin your read. They usually give you the opportunity for two takes. Do exactly what you are told and give them your best shot.

Have your business cards and extra demo tapes with you and hand them out freely to any new people you meet in the studio. Be happy, cooperative, and professional, and maybe wonderful things will happen!

At the end of your audition they will thank you and tell you approximately when they will be deciding on the talent and when you will be notified. Sometimes they will notify you if you *didn't* get the job, but usually they will notify just the chosen talent. The studio and especially the client will not appreciate numerous phone calls inquiring about the audition. Patience! When they tell you "Don't call me, we'll call you" they mean it! In fact, you will sleep better if you just forget the audition ever happened. If you got the job, believe me when I tell you they *will* find you!

When a closed audition call comes in, do everything in your power to get in on it. These are usually the "few and far between" gigs that could do a lot for your career. My best audition call came when I was down hard with the flu, hurling and trying to die. The studio manager said this was a once-in-a-lifetime opportunity, especially for this area, and I absolutely *had* to be at the studio in two hours. I was home sick from my air shift at the station because I was so violently ill, but I guess the show goes on. I dragged my poor little body down there, looking and feeling like swamp scum and proceeded with the audition as best I could. Much to my total amazement, I got the job! I landed a two-year run on national television anchoring a weekly entertainment segment for the *National Enquirer*.

Auditions are nerve-wracking. Do all you can to calm those nerves and make life a little easier. Do not overdose on caffeine. Find a professional outfit to wear that makes you feel good. The client is usually the business type, so a tie for the guys and a business suit for the gals goes a long way in how you represent yourself.

Allow lots of time to get to the studio even if you end up sitting in the car for a while. Minimize other activities going on so you can keep your focus. Breathe. Have fun and be grateful for such a special opportunity. You have worked hard to get this far and it is a real honor to receive a personal invitation to partake in an audition. It tells you someone has faith in your ability! Use that to boost your confidence and you will do just fine.

As you head into that audition, keep in mind your life does not depend on getting this one job! This helps you to relax and do your best work. Don't get discouraged if you do not win the audition. Not everyone can and there will be others. Don't take it personally. You may simply not have been the right character or personality type for the role. It does not mean you won't be absolutely perfect for the next one that comes along! And just think of the new contacts and all the experience you have gained by surviving another audition!

① ③

Setting Up Your Business

SETTING UP YOUR BUSINESS

YOUR OFFICE

Setting up a work area for your voiceover business is simple. A desk area with a bookshelf and a file drawer is all the space you will need. You will also be way ahead of the game if you own a personal computer. I have found this to be the one tool I would not want to do without.

The office supplies are basic and few. You will need:

A telephone
A business phonebook
A good quality answering machine
A pager
Business cards
Personalized postcards
Personalized stationery and envelopes
Package mailers
Printed labels
Stamps
File folders
Pens, pencils, and highlighters
Invoices
An accounting book or accounting software
A travel/mileage log
Index cards and file box
A cassette recorder
An appointment/date/address book

BUSINESS CARDS AND LETTERHEAD

In the beginning stages of your business, set yourself up with printed paper supplies. You will need business cards, letterhead, postcards, envelopes and mailing labels. There are lots of specialty papers on the market and they greatly contribute to a very handsome and coordinated appearance. You can find these on the shelves of office supply stores or through mail order. A much larger selection of designs will be through the mail order houses. Some of the best include:

Paper Direct	800-A-PAPERS
Paper Access	800-PAPER-01
Paper Showcase	800-842-3371
Queblo	800-523-9080

If you have a computer with a desktop publishing program and a decent inkjet printer you can design all your art work yourself. You can even do all your printing in your home and save on outside costs. I find this extremely convenient, especially if you change your phone number or address. Simply go into your program, make the changes and print up new stock. You have your new cards or letterhead in minutes instead of traipsing off to the printer and waiting three days for new stock...to say nothing of the added expense. I also tend to get tired of the same designs and like a change from time to time. This is a convenient, low-cost way of doing it.

A scanner is also a huge help when it comes to logo design. If you like to get creative you can make good use of one of the many good quality, moderately priced scanners on the market.

If you do not own a computer, you will need to find a printer with the skills and prices that suit your needs. Shop around. They can offer suggestions for design and a logo. They have thousands of graphics from which to choose and can guide you as to color, quality, layout, etc. There are lots of graphic artists around who design logos if you want to jazz up your look with your own unique design. Logos add a lot of pizzazz and professionalism if done well.

A special note about business cards. You may want to consider printing only your phone numbers on your cards and omit your mailing address. Your card will be handed out like candy and you really do not want Slimey Joe Schmoe having your home address in his possession. There is no reason for anyone to know where you live, just how to get hold of you. My cards display my name, title, and phone numbers for my office, fax, pager, cell phone, and internet e-mail address.

INVOICES

You will be invoicing your clients for each voiceover job. The most efficient invoices can be found in an office supply store. Choose the double copy, carbonless style. This provides the client with a copy for his billing records and a copy for you for your bookkeeping and tax purposes. Using your computer, you can print your name and address at the top. If you are not using a computer, stick a return address mailing label at the top. Always carry invoices with you to voiceover jobs and fill out the invoice there. Leave the original copy with the client and keep the duplicate for your records. If you do not get paid at the recording session, make sure the invoice goes into an "accounts receivable" folder when you get home.

LABELS

You will need several different kinds of labels. Again, with a home computer this becomes a simple process. All you have to do is purchase blank label forms and print your own. If you are not using a computer, you may want to have your local printer do the work for you. They stock the basic label forms you will be needing. You will need audio cassette labels for your demo tapes, mailing labels with a return address for mailing your demo packages, and return address labels for your invoices.

FILES

Your filing system will be super simple. You will need a folder for accounts receivable, a folder for accounts paid and a folder for business expenses. Keep your unpaid invoices in a readily-accessible folder so you can collect on these in a timely manner. It is easy to forget a job if it is a month later and you are busy with other stuff. Once an invoice is paid, enter it in a ledger and then mark the invoice paid and place it in the "paid" folder. This greatly simplifies your work come tax time. Save all your business expense receipts in your "expenses" folder. Most of your expenses will be tax deductible, but you will need to keep accurate records in the event Uncle Sam wants a peek.

TRAVEL/MILEAGE LOG
Keep a mileage log in your car and keep good accurate records of mileage and travel expenses. Get receipts for everything, including gas and tolls. You will need this come tax time and without it, you will not be able to legally deduct anything for travel expenses.

INDEX CARDS AND FILE BOX
The index cards are for your contacts and follow-up records. This is discussed in greater detail in the earlier chapter entitled "Contact Follow-up." Use monthly index tabs to keep track of when it is time to do your follow-up calls. Every time there is a contact with a client, be sure to note it on the card. This way you will always be clear on what has transpired with that client, who your contact is, and what your current status is.

TELECOMMUNICATIONS
Fast and easy communication links are crucial to your work. So many times a job will come in and it is an "emergency." It must be done yesterday and simply cannot wait a moment longer. Naturally the next question is inevitably "Can you get here right now?" Well, if they cannot reach you "right now," guess what?

They call someone else for the job. Availability and quick accessibility are critical!

A telephone at your work station is vital. Invest in a good quality, reliable answering machine that is accessible from outside your home. Get in the habit of checking in frequently for messages. Your outgoing message should be another example of your fabulous voice! Think of it as another great opportunity to audition. If someone is calling to consider you for a job, they will have a sample of your voice whether you are home or not. Create a friendly, professional, well-structured message using good diction and expressive inflection. On your message, you should also give the caller your pager number so they can reach you faster. State whether it is a digital or voice pager. It is impossible to know and it is very frustrating to get an uninterpretable message on your beeper. If you do get a weird message, check in with your answering machine right away. They may have left you a voice message.

Return all calls as quickly as possible. These studios and clients do not want to spend a lot of time tracking down talent. They will simply call someone who is less aggravating to reach. A mobile phone is a nice convenience if you can afford it. When the beeper goes off and you are on the highway, it is not always at a convenient or safe place to stop and look for a phone.

APPOINTMENT BOOK

Invest in a good appointment book with a daily calendar, address section, and client business card section. This will become invaluable as you build your busi ness. Write down everything from appointments to directions to names of secretaries! Keep your book stocked with your business cards and invoices. This is your little mobile office. Keep it up to date and take it with you everywhere you go!

SETTING TALENT FEES

It's tough putting a dollar value on your voice, and setting your talent fee is a difficult area to generalize. There are so many variables due to market size, supply and demand of talent versus jobs, project budgets, etc. I will do my best to give you some guidelines but you will need to adapt them to your own situation. Remember that we are tackling the voiceover business from the medium market in the United States. The big cities differ tremendously from the quaint little cow towns in the Midwest. My suggestion to you is to be flexible.

You will charge different rates for different jobs, clients and studios. Typically, your top-of-the-line television or video production studio will pay far more than your local cable company. In fact, cable companies usually have a lot of voice work but they function on very tight budgets and so pay rather poorly. Therefore, it is a great courtesy when the cable company makes the effort to gather 2 or 3 spots to record to make the trip more worthwhile. In a medium market you can only expect between $25 and $40 per 30-second spot. That is the lowest paid voiceover you should ever be asked to do. That's not too shabby, however, when there are several spots to record and it only takes about 20 minutes of time.

The average fee for a 30-second television spot in an average video production studio in your average market is in the range of $75 to $100. The average fee for a 60-second radio spot may also fall within that range.

Again, these fees vary greatly depending on the client's budget.

Industrials and corporate video narration are more negotiable. Some voice talents like to set an hourly fee, a page fee, or a total video running time fee. In my experience, the budgets behind these productions vary tremendously and I will try to work within their budget. Usually it is better than not doing the job at all!

When negotiating an industrial, or any job for that matter, do not get trapped into being the first to state a fee. When the studio or client calls and asks what you would charge for a job I will turn it around and ask what kind of budget they are working with. By giving a price first you may either underestimate your value or scare the client away forever. When you inquire about their budget they almost *always* come back with a figure. Now your job is much easier. If you feel that their figure is fair, let them know and it is now a done deal. If you feel it is too low, tell them tactfully that the fee you usually get paid for this type of job is just a touch more. At that point you must give them your lowest figure that you feel is fair. If it is *you* they want, most of the time they will accept it. If you feel you just cannot work for their price, let them know. They will soon find out they get what they pay for!

Use caution when setting industrial fees according to the quantity of pages before you see the script. They could tell you the script is ten pages. Ten pages could mean a lot of different things. The copy could be set up in what is known as storyboard format, where the words are typed double-spaced down the right half of the page. If you compressed that it would take up only about a quarter of a page. Or the copy could be single-spaced in very small typeface with very skinny margins. In the first case scenario it would take about 40 seconds to read. The second scenario would take about three minutes to read. Big difference! Never quote a fee based on pages before you have seen it.

You may want to give a fee based on the total running time of the narrated video. If you are reading for a ten minute video, maybe you will want to charge something in the range of $20 per minute of finished audio, or $200 for the job. Sometimes there will be a set fee up front...take it or leave it. They may say the video will be fifteen minutes in length and they are offering $300 for the job. Well, you really don't know if the video will be exactly fifteen minutes and it takes longer to actually record a video that length, but that is good pay for an hour of work! Another time you could be asked to read for a ten minute video and they will ask you if $800 would cover it! Try not to scream with delight...it's tacky. Simply state graciously that you feel it is very fair and you would love to do the job. Set it up, hang up the phone...and now you can scream. Remember a non-profit child abuse foundation will have a much smaller operating budget than NASA.

If a fee comes in that is much smaller than what you would like, see if you can negotiate a deal with the client. Ask if there might be more work down the road and can you have that work if you cut them a great deal on your fee now. Sometimes that is an effective way to secure future work and they will budget in a larger fee for your next session with them. If you do them a favor now they will probably try to compensate later.

You may want to consider giving a price break when the client has three or more spots for you. If you are being paid $75 per sixty-second spot and they have 6 spots, you could charge perhaps $400 instead of $450. If it is a good client that uses you regularly, maybe you will want to charge only $50 per spot when they group them together. $300 is still great pay for only an hour's work!

Fee-setting is a subjective negotiating process. Once you start working for the same studios, they know what you expect and they will secure that for you up front when dealing with their clients. Use caution when quoting a price for unseen work. When you are trying to secure new clients, be fair and flexible *without* just giving your voice away. After all, this is business.

COLLECTIONS

This is the part most of us hate to do. It's so pleasant when you just get a check on the spot and you do not have to deal with it further. Unfortunately, that is not the way it is usually done. Adopting a C.O.D. philosophy will probably put you out of business. Usually you leave an invoice with the studio or client, go home and wait for your check. Only sometimes you wait and wait and wait. It is fair to be paid within 30 days. Beyond 30 days it is time to place a reminder phone call or send another invoice. This can be frustrating, especially when you are spending time and money on collecting maybe only $35. But you have earned it and they are using your voice, so you have got to go after it. Be your sweet wonderful self when contacting them. You will usually see results after a reminder. As time goes on you can get firmer in your demand for payment. I have been stiffed for a job only once. Not bad odds for more than a decade in business.

In your larger markets, unions come into play. AFTRA (the American Federation of Television and Radio Artists) and SAG (Screen Actors Guild) are the two unions that encompass voiceover artists. The union-affiliated voiceover talent plays by a whole different set of rules. If you find yourself in a large market, look into your local union chapters for membership fees and requirements. You will need to join a union to get steady work and the big jobs. Your fees and payment would then be regulated by the union. Small market union-affiliation could be professional suicide!

BOOKKEEPING AND TAX OBLIGATIONS

Accurate bookkeeping is essential and it can be kept extremely simple. If you are not using a computer, a ledger is all you need. If you do have a computer, any simple accounting program can do most of the work for you. However you *do* need to remember to plug in the data! Any bookkeeping system is only as accurate as its entries.

The basic items you will need to enter are income and expenses. That's easy. When you receive payment for a voiceover job, enter the date, source, and the amount. In another column enter your business-related expenses, including the date, point of purchase and amount. Keep all receipts in a folder for tax time. Be sure to keep your travel log in your car and make entries as you go. Do not leave anything to memory!

Most of your clients will send you a *1099* statement at the beginning of the year for tax purposes, summarizing your total income from that source for the previous year. If you have worked for twelve clients, you can expect twelve 1099's. However, if your total earned from one client is under $600, they are not required to send one. This does not relieve you of the tax obligation, though. The 1099 indicates that you were an "independent contractor" and taxes have not been deducted. These must be claimed as part of your annual income and the appropriate taxes paid by April 15th. If you make a certain amount per year, quarterly estimates must be paid. Otherwise you can file annually with your other income. Be sure to check at what level of income you need to switch to quarterly taxes. I hesitate to quote you the current amount as it is subject to change. If you have been fortunate enough to be able to file just 1040's, be prepared to expand into Schedule C and Schedule SE on next year's tax return. The good news is when you are just beginning your business, you probably will not make enough to cause any super complicated tax returns. The better news is when your business is booming, you can afford to hire an accountant to figure it all out!

Because you are now considered self-employed with your freelance voiceover business, you are also entitled to business deductions. Pick up a booklet from your local tax office that spells out what you can and cannot deduct. Keep careful records and keep all receipts. These deductions will make a huge difference in your taxes.

14

Marketing & Promotion

MARKETING AND PROMOTION

What good does it do to have a great voice, great talent and a great demo package if nobody knows you exist? The marketing aspect of your voiceover business is just as important as your demo tape. One without the other renders everything useless. Good marketing and promotion is the last step you have to take to ensure yourself lucrative work in the voiceover industry.

YOUR MISSION: FLOOD THE MARKET WITH YOUR DEMO AND YOUR NAME!

YOUR MARKETING PACKAGE

You have gone through great efforts to put your demo tape together. Now you need to create your marketing package. This will include your demo tape, business card, cover letter and mailer envelope or box.

A cover letter is your tool of introduction. It states who you are and the purpose of your appearance. It defines your goal which is to acquire voiceover work. It tells the recipient exactly what is included in the package. It specifies what you expect of him or her and that is to give the tape a listen. It also says what your next move will be which is a follow-up call in the next few days. Your cover letter should be on matching or coordinating stationery and professionally typed or printed. Address it to a specific person by name, not "to whom it may concern." You have taken the time in your cold calling to studios to identify the person responsible for booking talent. Now you want to address that person by name. The letter should be brief, friendly and to the point. It is a tendency of the recipient to place the letter aside for later if it looks like it will take too much time to read right now. If it is just a couple of quick, neatly-written paragraphs they will be more inclined to give it immediate attention.

Your mailing envelope or box has to be appealing and attractive. Your package should have an "open me first" look all over it. It should make the recipient curious and anxious to open it. This is achieved by using good quality products, design and color. Your mailing label can have color and character to it and again, should be typed or printed and addressed to the specific individual who does the booking.

When it comes time to put your package in the mail, head on down to the post office. It's very tacky to put 8 stamps across the top of your envelope because you are too lazy or busy to mail it the proper way. Get off your duff and beat feet down to the local P.O.

Here are some check points you should consider:

- Use good quality bubble or padded envelopes if your demo is on a single cassette. Your demo tape should be in a plastic cassette case inside the mailer along with your cover letter. Get mailers large enough to accommodate the cover letter so that it is not folded up 8 times. You want your cover letter flat, folded in half or in thirds, and no more! Under no circumstances should you mail your tape in a standard letter envelope. It will be torn and tattered by the time it arrives and will scream of unprofessionalism.

- If your demo is on several cassettes inside a book-type case, you will need mailing boxes. These cost a little more than envelopes but the impression it makes is well worth it. They are book-size white cardboard boxes that need to be folded into shape, loaded with your tape case and letter, taped with clear packing tape, and labeled. They look very sharp and tend to stir up that "open me first" emotion I referred to earlier. It makes them feel like they are receiving a present.

- Flood the market with your voice demo. Hand these puppies out like candy to anyone and everyone who could end up getting you voice work. People move around like crazy and network frequently with other professionals. Word always gets around and so should your tapes! Promote yourself wherever you deem it appropriate. *Always* have demo tapes and business cards with you!

- We are in the midst of a fast and furious burst of the computer age and so let us not forget or ignore the cyber route. The internet is becoming a popular and convenient way to market your voice. Sites have been set up that can showcase your voice samples along with other talent. A client simply logs on and listens to available talent. Other voice talents have set up their own web pages that advertise their voiceover business and offer samples of their voice. Their demo tape is right there for the world to hear with the click of a mouse. It is usually linked to an e-mail box to accommodate inquiries.

- Print advertising is an option if your budget allows it. You will always see ads for voice talent in the radio trade publications such as *Radio & Records*, but they are not cheap! It is rare that you will see that type of ad in local classifieds, though. It is a costly proposition but one you may want to consider once you are established and successful. In the beginning, however, your personal one-on-one contacts will get you better results.

① ⑤

Practice Copy Samples

PRACTICE COPY SAMPLES

The following pages feature some samples of commercial copy that have actually been used on the air at one time or another.

Use these for practice. Time yourself and adjust your pacing to finish precisely at the designated time. Some are straight forward 60-second spots, 30-second spots, and others taken from jingle or donut spots. The specific read time will be indicated at the top. Use a stopwatch or second hand and practice reading through them until you get the proper pacing. Use your cassette recorder and do several takes with several different types of reads. Picture a specific type of listener, or demographic, for each read and vary it accordingly. Listen back carefully, as self-critique is crucial for improvement.

Feel free to use any of this copy on your demo tape. You will not be using the whole spot, as explained in the chapter on making your demo tape. You will only be using about 10 seconds of each. It is a good idea to use national copy on your demo. It gives you a "bigger" image than if you used copy for Al's Pawn Shop down on Main Street.

SPOT 1   :60   WONDER BREAD

Have you tried Wonder Bread lately? Wonder's new extra baking step makes it better than ever! It's firmer and full-bodied...even more tender...but spreadable. It's got a richer, deeper flavor. Toasts great, too. Now Wonder even seems to stay fresher longer. And mothers...during the "Wonder Years", the formative years, ages one through twelve, your child develops in many ways...actually grows to 90% of his adult height. When you serve Wonder Bread during the Wonder Years, you supply your child with protein for muscle, minerals for bones and teeth, carbohydrates for energy, and vitamins for nerves. Yes, Wonder supplies all these vital elements for growing minds and bodies. So to help make the most of their Wonder Years...their growth years. Serve Wonder Enriched Bread. Wonder Bread helps build strong bodies 12 ways. And remember, Wonder is made a new way with an extra step, so it tastes better than ever. Have you tried Wonder Bread lately?

SPOT 2   :60   TWA'S AMBASSADOR EXPRESS

TWA introduces the first sane, sensible way to take a short business flight to Chicago. TWA's Ambassador Express. If you can't get your ticket in advance, now you can buy it right at the departure gate. Hate waiting for your bags? TWA is putting new luggage compartments on many of its Ambassador Express flights, so you'll be able to bring even full-size bags with you right on board. TWA is re-doing the interiors of their planes...first class and coach. You used to sit three across in coach. Now if they're not full, you'll find TWA's new twin seat. Food? On meal flights, TWA gives you a choice...a full meal or a light snack. TWA's new Ambassador Express from Hartford to Chicago. It's what thousands of businessmen and women have always wanted, expected and deserved from a short business flight. TWA's Ambassador Express from Hartford to Chicago. Flights at noon and 4 PM daily. Service begins April 15. All planes completed by mid-summer.

SPOT 3   :30   EXCEDRIN

If there's an occasional cold in the neighborhood and you've got aspirin, you're pretty well prepared...to get *some* relief from the aches and pain and fever. But now there's a flu epidemic. What you and your family really want is Excedrin. For aches and pains of a cold or flu, Excedrin does everything aspirin can do. Excedrin has *two* effective fever reducers...and Excedrin has an anti-depressant. When you feel that low down and weary, every little bit can help. Tablet for tablet, Excedrin is 50% stronger than aspirin for pains that come with colds and flu. Excedrin...the extra-strength pain reliever.

SPOT 4   :30   GOODYEAR AUTO SERVICE

You asked for quality auto service at affordable sale prices, and Goodyear Retailers listened! That's why right now, they're offering big savings on Goodyear Certified Auto Service! For a limited time, an oil change, chassis lube and filter is sale-priced for just $14.95! Goodyear's Cooling System Radiator Protection Service is on sale right now for only $9.95! But only through December 31st...so hurry to an authorized Goodyear Certified Auto Service location today, before it's too late...and save! Nobody fits you like Goodyear.

SPOT 5   :22 DONUT   BACHMAN GOLDEN

If you're looking for a way to brighten up your day, think golden...Bachman Golden Ridges and Golden Crisp Potato Chips! 'Cause Bachman's got a special way with snacks. And Golden Ridges and Golden Crisp Potato Chips are no exception. So light and so crispy delicious, they're simply irresistible. Bachman Golden Ridges and Golden Crisp Potato Chips. What a golden way to make friends!

SPOT 6   :20 JINGLE   INSERT   DOMINO'S PIZZA

Don't settle for a dull boring job! Call Domino's Pizza and check out management and driver opportunities! You can enjoy a rewarding career by becoming a part of the world's largest pizza delivery company. From in-store operations to area supervisor, Domino's Pizza provides the upward mobility you're looking for. Domino's Pizza is looking for bright, ambitious people...so call Domino's Pizza...now!

❶❻

Leaving The Nest

LEAVING THE NEST

There comes a time in all our lives when our mom shoves us out of our comfortable and secure nest. Well, I sure hope you are ready to fly because for you, that time is now. You have been nurtured and taught the ways of the voiceover world. The time is here to discover it for yourself.

Remember that building a new business takes time. You probably have lots of other work and activity going on in your life while trying to establish yourself in voice work. Be kind to yourself and don't go too crazy trying to do it all in one day! It is best to set reasonable goals and then attempt to meet them. If you send out thirty demos in one day, how could you possibly do proper follow-up? Remember the section on pacing? Try it here, too. If you send out five demos a week for six weeks, you will be able to manage your business and your life much more efficiently.

If you choose to follow the majority of the advice presented in this voiceover kit and you have some degree of talent and ambition, you now have a very exciting future to look forward to! You will meet so many great people along the way. If it really takes off, no two days will be the same to you anymore. You will appreciate far more diversity and unpredictability in your life. You will enjoy the new surprises that this business inherently brings into your day-to-day living. It will add new sparkle to a dull, boring, and predictable life.

If you have been practicing on a regular basis you really should be feeling fairly confident by now. It may be a good idea to have another professional in the field listen to your practice cassette and give critique on your work. Do not even bother asking friends or family, because unless you are in the middle of a family feud they will probably say you are wonderful. That will not help to improve your skills. It may be nice to hear but friends and family do tend to be a pit partial.

I want to leave you with a reminder I mentioned earlier in the book. Never, never become complacent with your skills. You can always become a better voiceover talent. Even when you are getting a good quantity of work coming in, you must strive to keep your skills sharper than the next guy. Take those extra acting or improv classes. They will add so much depth to your performance.

If you feel that you have benefited from *Put Your Mouth Where The Money Is*, I would love to hear from you! I have assisted in training hundreds of talented folks just like you and always appreciate hearing a good all-American success story!

I do want to wish you the very best this business has to offer. From this day forward, may you lead an interesting and exciting life...and make a heck of a good living from your radio and television voiceover career.

Above all, be happy.

INDEX

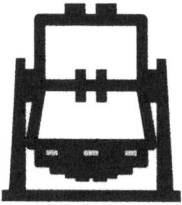

Voiceovers from A to Z

INDEX

BOOK ORDER FORM

To order **PUT YOUR MOUTH WHERE THE MONEY IS!**
please send check or money order to: Airwave Publications
(Allow 3 weeks for delivery if paying by check)   P.O. Box 753
                                                    Jupiter, Florida 33468-0753

OR charge ○ Visa   ○ Mastercard   ○ Discovery   ○ AMEX
Card Number:_____
Name on card:_____ Exp: ____/____
Signature: _____

OR E-mail the requested information to: sunnyq@juno.com
OR Order through the internet at http://www.airwav.com

Please send my book(s) to:

Name: (Please Print) _____

Address: _____

City:_____ State:_____ Zip:_____

Phone: (In case of question about your order) (_____)_____

Quantity _____ @ $49.95 each   Total Price: _____

(If ordering up to 3 books,   Shipping: _____<u>4.95</u>
you still pay only $4.95.
$2.00 per book thereafter) Additional shipping if applicable: _____

   Florida shipping addresses ONLY, add 6% Sales Tax: _____

                                   Total Enclosed: _____

You have a 10-day money back satisfaction guarantee! If you are not happy with your purchase, your money will be refunded (shipping expenses exempt).

Thank you! Your order will be shipped immediately!

BOOK ORDER FORM

To order **PUT YOUR MOUTH WHERE THE MONEY IS!**
please send check or money order to: Airwave Publications
(Allow 3 weeks for delivery if paying by check) P.O. Box 753
Jupiter, Florida 33468-0753

OR charge ○ Visa   ○ Mastercard   ○ Discovery   ○ AMEX
Card Number:_____
Name on card:_____ Exp: ____/____
Signature: _____

OR E-mail the requested information to: sunnyq@juno.com
OR Order through the internet at http://www.airwav.com

Please send my book(s) to:

Name: (Please Print) _____

Address: _____

City:_____ State:_____ Zip:_____

Phone: (In case of question about your order) (_____)_____

Quantity _____ @ $49.95 each   Total Price: _____

(If ordering up to 3 books,   Shipping: _____4.95
you still pay only $4.95.
$2.00 per book thereafter) Additional shipping if applicable: _____

Florida shipping addresses ONLY, add 6% Sales Tax: _____

Total Enclosed: _____

You have a 10-day money back satisfaction guarantee! If you are not happy with your purchase, your money will be refunded (shipping expenses exempt).

Thank you! Your order will be shipped immediately!

BOOK ORDER FORM

To order **PUT YOUR MOUTH WHERE THE MONEY IS!**
please send check or money order to: Airwave Publications
(Allow 3 weeks for delivery if paying by check)   P.O. Box 753
Jupiter, Florida 33468-0753

OR charge ◯ Visa   ◯ Mastercard   ◯ Discovery   ◯ AMEX
Card Number:_____
Name on card:_____ Exp: ____ / ____
Signature: _____

OR E-mail the requested information to: sunnyq@juno.com
OR Order through the internet at http://www.airwav.com

Please send my book(s) to:

Name: (Please Print) _____

Address: _____

City:_____ State:_____ Zip:_____

Phone: (In case of question about your order) (_____)_____

Quantity _____ @ $49.95 each   Total Price: _____

(If ordering up to 3 books,   Shipping: _____ <u>4.95</u>
you still pay only $4.95.
$2.00 per book thereafter) Additional shipping if applicable: _____

Florida shipping addresses ONLY, add 6% Sales Tax: _____

Total Enclosed: _____

You have a 10-day money back satisfaction guarantee! If you are not happy with your purchase, your money will be refunded (shipping expenses exempt).

Thank you! Your order will be shipped immediately!

 Notes

 **Notes**